Assessment and
for lang

Centre for Information
on Language Teaching and Research

The Centre for Information on
Language Teaching and Research
provides a complete range of services
for language professionals in every
stage and sector of education, and in
business, in support of its brief to
promote Britain's foreign language
capability.

CILT is a registered charity, supported
by Central Government grants. CILT
is based in Covent Garden, London,
and its services are delivered through
a national collaborative network of
regional Comenius Centres in
England, the National Comenius
Centre of Wales, Scottish CILT and
Northern Ireland CILT.

CILT Publications are available
through all good booksellers or
directly from:

Grantham Book Services Ltd
Isaac Newton Way
Alma Park Industrial Estate
Grantham, Lincs NG31 8SD
Telephone: 01476 541 080
Fax: 01476 541 061

Assessment & Accreditation for languages

The emerging consensus?

Edited by Anke Hübner,
Toni Ibarz and Sara Laviosa

CiLT
Centre for Information
on Language Teaching and Research

THE UNIVERSITY
OF BIRMINGHAM

The views expressed in this publication are the author's and do not necessarily represent those of CILT.

First published 2000

ISBN 1 902031 23 7

A catalogue record for this book is available from the British Library

Printed in Great Britain by Copyprint UK Ltd

Published by the Centre for Information on Language Teaching and Research, 20 Bedfordbury, Covent Garden, London WC2N 4LB

CILT Publications are available from: Grantham Book Services, Isaac Newton Way, Alma Park Industrial Estate, Grantham, Lincs NG31 8SD. Tel: 01476 541 080. Fax: 01476 541 061. Book trade representation (UK and Ireland): Broadcast Book Services, 2nd Floor, 248 Lavender Hill, London SW11 1JL. Tel: 020 7924 5615. Fax: 020 7924 2165.

Contents

Introduction

The teaching of modern languages in university departments of continuing education: credits, credentials and credibility

Toni Ibarz, University of Sheffield

In June 1997, under the auspices of the Department of Continuing Education of the University of Nottingham, a group of linguists met for a one day conference to discuss accreditation. There were 45 participants, mostly from universities but also representatives of the further education sector, mostly full-time but also part-time language tutors, the majority working in England and some in Scotland. The theme of the conference was: assessment and accreditation of foreign language courses in university departments of continuing education (CE), with the title: *Assessment and accreditation for foreign languages: the emerging consensus?*. The organisers went under the banner of UACE Linguists, a small group of professionals in the area of HE foreign language teaching/learning whose job profile did not fit into any of the existing organisations. They therefore felt the need to create a network in order to respond to a particular set of circumstances, namely the need to accredit courses which hitherto had been part of a liberal adult education tradition which had not favoured any type of accreditation. The papers included in this publication are the result of research conducted either in relation to the process of introducing formal assessment methods or to the need to explore the potential for innovation. This introductory paper has as its aim to encourage discussion around the role and purpose of a group of linguists which, it is argued, have something original to contribute to both the university adult education setting in which they work and to their colleagues in the world of language teaching.

The points made here are complemented with background on the context and constituency of UACE Linguists and with the results of two surveys on the provision of modern languages in university continuing education which will be found in the last paper of this publication: 'Measuring the impact of accreditation: two surveys on the provision of modern languages in university departments of continuing education'. The surveys show that the aims of UACE Linguists in the area of accreditation were realised and that several departments are already in the process of revising and refining their assessment and accreditation programmes.

The Nottingham Conference had as one of its purposes to encourage the members of UACE Linguists to begin to formulate a research agenda in line with the latest demands made on staff working in the university sector. Therefore, successes in the area of accreditation and the encouraging developments in the area of research may lead to some complacency. However, in the present climate of change, all the signs are that any complacency would be naive. The provision of modern languages in universities is a complex affair in which the politics and economy of language teaching come into play with the role and relevance given in each institution to departments of CE. Recently, several universities have rearranged their language provision, often reaching very different conclusions. For example, two similar neighbouring universities which have taken part in the two surveys mentioned above went through this process. One transferred their language courses from the department of CE to the mainstream languages department, the other transferred languages courses from the languages teaching unit into the department of CE.

There is uncertainty as to the future of modern languages in university departments of CE and it can be argued that it does not matter which part of the university is offering modern language courses to the local community. Most would agree that the main consideration is that universities open their door to the public and that they offer a variety of language courses which satisfy the needs of the population in its surrounding area. Some would like a further refinement and would insist on seeing the opportunity to take part in such programmes offered to the social groups which have traditionally been underrepresented in universities (Ainslie and Sargant, quoted in Arthur, 1996). There are perhaps more than 250 institutions nationwide offering what can be loosely classed as modern languages in HE and the OU is fast gaining relevance as a provider of language courses with over 4000 students in French alone. Does it matter if the courses are offered by CE departments? What is distinctive about languages in CE departments? What should distinguish languages in CE and languages in other departments of the universities? What does CE offer that is not offered by FE and other AE providers?

The brief attempt in the next few paragraphs to generate discussion around possible answers has no intention to claim that any of the points made apply exclusively to CE departments, hopefully it will become apparent that the only possible originality is the way in which they combine and the space they offer for potential development. The points made come under five headings:

1	**2**	**3**	**4**	**5**
Two cultures	The 'great tradition'	Europe	Approach to accreditation and teaching	Research

Two cultures

Mainly for historical reasons, most UACE linguists work in a faculty of education. This means that their professional lives are immersed in two cultures with different discourses. With part-time tutors and with students they may use the language of ALL (Association for Language Learning) and CILT (Centre for Information in Language Teaching and Research), but with their departmental colleagues they use the language of UACE (University Association for Continuing Education), which is often closer to the world of education and the social sciences. This may account for the sense of isolation that had occasionally been mentioned in the surveys and for the difficulties experienced with some administrative and academic colleagues when explaining and discussing proposed models of accreditation. How many times has the question been heard: 'why do languages have to be different?' The reverse is also true. Most UACE linguists have trained as applied linguists and teachers of modern languages and see themselves as linguists first and 'educators' second, and are not always comfortable in some of the discussions that take place in their departments. There is obviously no attempt to indicate that there is a real contradiction between the two discourses. It is a convenient division which may help to highlight in the next few paragraphs, that this 'biculturalism' which can be seen by some as problematic, could instead be grasped as an opportunity for developing distinctive teaching and research which benefit from having the support of a multidisciplinary environment.

The 'great tradition'

As has just been indicated, many language teachers in CE have trained and developed professionally in very different educational environments and sometimes may be surprised to find out that university departments of CE are part of a long tradition of liberal adult education — education for personal development — that started in the nineteenth century:

> The particular type of LAE offered by university departments was defined as a 'great tradition' by Harold Wiltshire (1956). This 'great tradition' was given a number of defining characteristics: a commitment to humane/liberal studies; an especial concern for social studies as a way of understanding the great issues of modern life; a non-vocational attitude; a non-selective provision which has democratic notions of the educability of adults; an adoption of the Socratic method in its use of small tutorial groups and guided discussion. (Ambrose, 1995: 17)

The origins go back to the Oxford and Cambridge extension studies centres, some of which later became the 'redbrick' universities, with lectures on economics, politics and history. A movement that developed and was radicalised in the early part of this century with the formation of the WEA (Workers' Educational Association) in 1903, '*a new organisation to unite the interests of universities and the working-classes*' (Ambrose,1995; 8). It is interesting to note that it proposed the 'tutorial class' as the means to educate the masses. Joseph Roper, in his memoirs of the partnership between the WEA and Sheffield University, describes the main features of such courses:

> *The classes were requested by self-forming groups of students. They committed themselves to a progressive course of three years in one subject. The tutor was appointed by the University but, in theory at least, was approved by the students. As Board of Education grants were involved there was a rather tight set of Regulations governing the obligations of tutors and students. For grant purposes students were required to make two-thirds of the attendances at the twenty four meetings per session. There was a requirement of written work set, by convention at twelve essays each session. The class was to run with a one hour lecture and one hour for discussion. The relaxed atmosphere of the Oxford tutorial was the teaching method for the tutorial class. It was, however, a difficult ideal to sustain under the stringent requirements of the Regulations, the intrinsic difficulties of unselected recruitment and "all-age-group" membership, together with the contingencies of workers' lives. (Roper, 1993: 10)*

Much of what he says has resonances for the modern reader. The concern about teaching methods and student involvement was already there, as was the tension between bureaucracy and pedagogy. It is the same tradition that was behind the creation of the extramural departments, later to become CE departments and perhaps soon to be called centres for lifelong learning. The same tradition that informs many aspects of the recent report of the National Advisory Group for Continuing Education and Lifelong Learning which may have significant influence on government policy:

> *...the publication of a white paper on lifelong learning represents a major opportunity for the government to set out its vision of a culture of lifelong learning for all. Learning must become normal and accessible, and learners must be put at the centre, taking increased ownership of their own learning and its management throughout life. Variety and diversity of learning opportunities is key...*

Having an understanding of the 'second culture' may, therefore, make an important contribution towards a sense of distinctiveness and perhaps will ensure greater relevance if some of the proposed new opportunities for adults become a reality. There are also voices coming from within the world of language learning who express similar concerns. Statements like the ones above are often heard in discussions on active learning and learner centredness. For example, Tudor (1996: xi) in a recent book that translates much of what could be seen as part of the 'great tradition' into a linguist's discourse, writes:

> *...the view of language teaching upon which this book rests involves the belief that education, in whatever field, should seek to provide students not only with discrete knowledge and skills, but also with the capacity to operate in an informed and self-directive manner in the skill area in question, within the wider context of their chosen life goals. In this perspective, education is seen as a means of empowerment. This argument clearly has a social dimension, since it recognises that language learners are members of a social group, and views language education as a means of enabling them to fulfil their language-related life goals within this group in a constructive and socially responsible manner.*

Europe

The 'great tradition' has also had its European dimension and as linguists it may be worthwhile to note that, for example, several of the influential studies on which many present day language programmes and accreditation systems are still based, were developed as part of the Council of Europe programmes on adult and permanent / continuing education in the early seventies by experts like Trim, Van Ek, Wilkins, Holec and others. In the introduction to the *Threshold Level English* (p3), Van Ek writes:

> *The accumulated expertise and experience of the government officials, representatives of organisations of adult education, teachers and researchers assembled at these symposia has formed the foundation on which the project rests.*

The 'pioneering' role of adult education extended also into other areas, as acknowledged, for example, by David Little (1996: 23):

> *Much of the current interest in learner autonomy arises from theories of adult education that came to prominence in the 1970s. Thus Autonomy and foreign language learning, Henri Holec's pioneering study (1981), takes as its starting point the argument that the purpose of adult education should be to prepare the individual learner for participation in the democratic process.*

And yet, it can be argued that, from the point of view of language learning, adult education has not figured prominently in many of the European programmes and that most CE departments have not benefited from European initiatives. We are also told by Trim and his colleagues that the recommendations for modern languages adopted by the Council for Cultural Co-operation were based on such beliefs as:

> • *that linguistic diversity was part of the European cultural heritage and that it should, through the study of modern languages, provide a source of intellectual enrichment rather than an obstacle to unity;*
>
> • *that only if the study of modern European languages became*

> *general would full mutual understanding and co-operation be possible in Europe;*
>
> • *that a better knowledge of modern European languages would lead to the strengthening of links and the increase in international exchanges on which economic and social progress in Europe increasingly depends.*

(*Systems Development in Adult Language Learning*, 1973: 1)

Such statements may be seen as not much more than rhetoric, but they are in sharp contrast with the status of modern languages in adult education in general and in CE departments in particular. Languages are not always seen as an essential component for European citizenship and even when CE departments have links with other European institutions, often in the area of CVE, modern linguists are not included. Also, other language teaching sections of universities and other HE and FE institutions have benefited more from Europe than CE. As indicated earlier, it could be argued that the fault is not all with one side, it is very likely that UACE linguists could have been more aware of the larger picture and it may be a case of missed opportunities for research funding and for links and exchanges.

Approach to accreditation and teaching

The Nottingham Conference contained a question in the title: *Assessment and Accreditation for Languages: the emerging consensus?* which reflected the attempt by UACE Linguists to develop a system of credits based on modules of similar length and value which would allow mobility across departments and would allow future development in co-operation between departments. It soon became apparent that this would not be possible mainly because each institution had specific requirements and constraints. The exercise, however, was not futile and it ensured that the basic approach and the CATS/SCOTSCAT frameworks created established common characteristics across departments, as will become apparent from reading the papers of the conference. The assessment had to be non threatening to adult students and had to be integrated as much as possible into normal classroom activities in as formative a way as possible. It was also felt important that the process counted with the support of part-time tutors who were widely consulted.

The papers presented at the conference discuss aspects of assessment and accreditation in a way which shows that much exploratory work has already been done in this area. Departments hold a considerable amount of data on which to base the type of research that could be of use across the whole adult education sector. There is potential for co-operation with the Open College and other interested bodies. In addition to the topics covered by the papers presented at the conference, there is a broad spectrum of research being carried out in CE departments on topics like, for example: part-time tutor training and staff development, retention, motivation, placement and diagnostic tests, the role of the external examiners, and the challenge of incorporating learning strategies and analytical and critical skills into course syllabi.

Research

Looking at the responses to the second survey conducted by UACE Linguists, it was noticeable that several departments, in particular two in Scottish universities, were basing their replies on research and tutor and student questionnaires rather than simply on opinion. It appears that a culture of research is beginning to permeate the activities of several CE departments. This is one of the main distinguishing features between adult educators based in universities and those working in other sectors. On the one hand it is a question of professional survival, many of those involved in UACE Linguists need to comply with their contractual obligations, on the other hand research could offer departments of CE scope for a potential role in developments that could be of relevance beyond the strict confines of the RAE (Research Assessment Exercise) return forms.

As indicated above, UACE linguists share characteristics and interests with colleagues in a variety of institutions, many of which are research led. There is room for co-operation with them, they may want to have an adult education (AE) dimension to their research. However, it is likely that our contribution, however limited it may be, could have a greater impact if directed towards AE, a sector which often operates with very specific defining features and constraints: weak organisational structures, precarious conditions of employment, poor training and insufficient contact hours, and which is always in desperate need for informed/research led development in several of the areas mentioned in the previous paragraphs. We often compete with them for students but they could be our allies in the area of research.

UACE linguists work under considerable constraints, mainly time but also the ambiguity from the universities as to their research and their role in the RAE. Having a research agenda should be a helpful first step in trying to define a clear role. The potential seems to be there: it could be a case of joint projects with other departments or simply internal initiatives, perhaps involving the use of part-time tutors, some of whom are very highly qualified, they would follow an action research or a reflective practitioner approach, perhaps as part of their training, or postgraduate students or even research assistants could be involved. More ambitious projects could involve AE centres or even have a European dimension. Funding has, of course, to be sought, but the same applies to other disciplines and, with some consideration, the case for research on modern languages in AE could be made forcefully.

The papers presented at the Nottingham conference

Many of the points made in the section about the 'great tradition' were taken up by Liam Kane's stimulating paper *Language teaching, accreditation and the social purpose of adult education* where he seeks to place language teaching (in continuing education) into a wider adult education context, with a particular focus on the issue of adult education and social change. He looks briefly at the development of radical adult education in the UK and the ideas of Gramsci and Freire, and argues that as with other aspects of educational practice, there is no such thing as politically neutral language teaching and either by design or default, adult educators teaching modern languages are 'cultural workers' engaged in political activity: the key question to be addressed is what the nature of this activity ought to be. Arguing that adult education can and should be a force for social change, the paper addresses some of the methodological questions which this then raises for language teachers of adults. With reference to previous research, it goes on to examine the impact on accreditation on the potential of language teaching to contribute towards social change. It argues that for institutions seeking to promote an educational practice which goes beyond the straitjacket of vocationalism, there are ways of approaching accreditation which can do much to minimise the damage.

Fran Beaton's paper on *Student attitudes to learning, assessment and accreditation* describes a system of dual accreditation and the development of a user-friendly approach that enables students to work towards their personal goals, the development of professional language skills or HE. It examines the tensions which can arise between formal requirements, tutor perceptions and students' own interests and needs. It also focuses on the marked differences in attitude between EFL students and students in other foreign language courses and on ways to foster positive attitudes towards accreditation.

Dounia Bissar deals with issues related to a university wide programme open to undergraduate and adult part-time students: *Assessment on a fully accredited Open Language Programme: achieving beneficial backwash in a standardised scheme*. The paper presents the approach to assessment used in the Open Language Programme at the University of

North London as an illustrative case study in order to discuss the relationship between validity and reliability on the one hand and the demands for standardisation on the other. She argues that at times compromises have to be made. She also considers related issues like scaling, marking grids, communicative testing, etc.

Ian McCall, in *Introducing credit and assessment: attitudes and responses among adult language learners* begins by outlining the assessment scheme and the accreditation model introduced in his department. It then highlights how it was set up in such a way as to maximise student participation and how it was 'marketed' persuasively as essential to the learning experience. The second part discusses students' reactions to the scheme and how they perceived the effects of assessment on their learning experience. This part is based on data from a questionnaire completed by 268 respondents of all ages studying a broad range of popular and minority languages from beginners to advanced level.

Sara Laviosa in *Translation to assess language competence: present and future*, begins by analysing the way and the extent to which translation is currently used as a means of assessing language competence in adult learners at the Modern Languages Unit of the University of Birmingham. She then goes on to propose, on the basis of the insights provided by Translation Studies, that translation can be used not just to test lexical and grammatical accuracy, but, most importantly, as a means of assessing cultural and pragmatic competence in the foreign language.

Linda Hartley and Marion Spöring in *Communicative assessment for adult language learners: carrying coals to Newcastle?* begin by establishing that tutors, through lack of time or training, have difficulties in setting up appropriate communicative assessment tasks. In their paper they discuss and exemplify methods of communicative assessment used in two language programmes at the University of Dundee, one for adults and one for undergraduates.

In the final paper, *Assessment and accreditation of languages: implications for tutor training*, Anke Hübner describes a project which enquired into the training needs of part-time tutors. Several British and German institutions were surveyed and the results are presented in an organised and methodical way. The paper touches on some of the theoretical issues involved and makes a helpful contribution to the quality assurance debate by outlining a systematic appoach to identifying the training requirements of the ever growing community of hourly paid members of the teaching staff.

Conclusion

This conference has addressed one of the main challenges: the challenge of accreditation. There are many more. For example, rising financial pressures through reduced funding has led to increased competition among providers. The ensuing reduction in courses and the need for larger groups to make classes viable are detrimental to the interests of students and are a cause of time and resources wastage. There is a need for collaboration across providers to improve on the range of levels and languages on offer. What should the role of CE departments be in relation to other sectors? What is the best way to explore further the question of defining the identity of UACE linguists' language programmes in relation to those offered elsewhere? Should university CE strengthen its social purpose and attempt to continue to offer high quality language classes in the lesser taught and community languages? How can students from a wider social background be attracted? UACE Linguist have a distinctive contribution to make combining expertise as linguists with experience as adult educators in a research environment, but is research in CE departments a realistic possibility? Kennedy, Dearing, and Fryer's report on lifelong learning and ultimately the government's White Paper may create new challenges, but at the same time they will create new opportunities. Let us hope that this conference has pointed CE modern languages in the right direction.

Bibliography

Ambrose P, G Holloway and G Mayhew, *All change! Accreditation as a challenge to liberal adult education* (University of Sussex,1995)

Arthur L, 'Adults learning languages' in Hawkins E (ed) *30 years of language teaching* (CILT, 1996)

European Commission White Paper Teaching and Learning: towards the learning society (http://www.cec.lu/en/comm/dg22/dg22.html)

Holec H, *Autonomy and foreign language learning* (Pergamon Press, 1981)

Report of the National Advisory Group for Continuing Education and Lifelong Learning (Abridged and edited in *The Times Higher,* 28 November 1997)

Little D, 'Learner autonomy and learner counselling', in Little D and H Brammerts (eds) *A guide to language learning in tandem via the Internet*, CLCS Occasional Paper No 46 (Trinity College Dublin, 1996)

Roper J, *The challenge of adult education* (University of Sheffield, 1993)

Trim J L M et al, *Systems development in adult language learning* (Pergamon Press, 1973)

Tudor I, *Learner centredness as language education* (Cambridge University Press, 1996)

Van Ek J A and L G Alexander, *Threshold Level English* (Pergamon Press, 1975)

Language teaching, accreditation and the social purpose of adult education

1

Liam Kane, University of Glasgow

The fundamental, social purpose of adult education has long been a topic of debate. Surprisingly, however, given the number of students involved, its relation to the teaching of modern languages is seldom discussed. This article begins with a resumé of the debate, explores the potential contribution of language teaching to progressive social change, considers how this might be affected by recent moves towards accreditation and suggests ways of coping with potential complications.

The social purpose of adult education

Whatever is seen as the purpose of adult education — whether to boost economic production, improve individual well-being or try to change society, for example — it is fundamentally a political consideration, general in nature but applicable to all subject areas, with practical implications for teaching. Broadly speaking, there is a conservative, liberal and radical perspective. A conservative view champions capitalist economics and sees the role of education as both meeting the changing needs of the market and preserving the concept of 'traditional values': class differences are part of the natural order. A liberal view focuses on the individual and sees many reasons — class differentiation being one — which explain why people do not achieve their full potential. While not challenging the fundamental structure of society, liberal education will seek to compensate for any disadvantage, promoting equality of opportunity so that individuals are free to 'better themselves'. It also supports the humanistic concept of personal growth through education. This philosophy was preeminent before 1979 — when conservatism started to bite — and indeed, until fairly recently, the term 'liberal adult education' was still in common use.

A radical view sees social injustice as a product of capitalism, with formal education often — though not exclusively — playing the role of promoter of conservative values. It argues that education should help change society for the better and promotes collectivist rather than individualist values, encouraging critical analysis of society and a desire to take action for change. Since the time of the industrial revolution, Britain has had a rich history of organised, independent initiatives providing educational support for working class struggles though since the 1950s, the debate has mostly focused on education funded by the state (Westwood, 1992). Despite disorientation on the left and the increasing impact of postmodernist ideology, given the persistence of hardship and social problems in contemporary Britain, the radical agenda is unlikely to disappear (last year the government's own figures — collated by the Joseph Rowntree Foundation — showed that one in three babies in the UK is born into poverty; the United Nations Development Report confirmed the ever widening gap in Britain between the rich and poor) though it has broadened out from its immediate focus on class to include the concerns of, for example, feminist and anti-racist movements.

The best known advocates of radicalism have been Antonio Gramsci and Paulo Freire. Gramsci, a Marxist and founder member of the Italian Communist Party, was imprisoned by Mussolini and developed his educational ideas in his *Prison notebooks*. Arguing against the economic reductionism of orthodox Marxism he maintained that 'hegemony' — domination by consent — was an important factor in the ruling class's ability to keep control (in an updated version of Gramsci's thinking, Noam Chomsky uses the term 'Manufacturing Consent'). As hegemony is achieved through influencing the institutions of civil society — the church, education, the press, for example — Gramsci argued for the development of a 'counter-hegemonic' culture in which civil society became an important 'site of struggle' for social change. Radical education had an important role to play, therefore, and he was particularly keen on the concept of 'organic intellectuals', radical educators who would emerge from the working class free of the conservative ideological baggage of the traditional academic.

Whereas Gramsci was more a theorist on education's role in the struggle for change, Freire, a Brazilian, was a hands-on teacher who developed a method for putting radical education into practice. He has had an enormous impact on education worldwide, particularly through his *Pedagogy of the Oppressed*. He argues that in all contexts — whether in the 'third' or 'first' worlds — in all areas of knowledge, there is no such thing as politically neutral education: *'to wash your hands of the conflict between the powerful and the powerless is to side with the powerful, not to be neutral'* (Freire, 1973:1). Freire criticised what he called 'banking education', the notion that education is about wise teachers 'depositing' superior knowledge into the empty minds of learners. He called for a dialogue between teachers and learners in which together they analyse the social reality of which they are part. Crucially, education should encourage learners to take action to change their world though an important distinction from a traditional left-wing approach is that people should not be made dependent on leaders but should themselves become 'subjects', not 'objects', of change. Ideally, action should lead to collective organisation.

Freire's approach to teaching literacy was particularly acclaimed. People learn skills of social analysis — 'reading the world' — at the same time as learning letters and words. Instead of starting with 'A, B, C . . .' learners begin by discussing issues important to their lives and then learn the words most relevant to their situation (so literacy classes might begin with the word 'refugee' or 'land', for example). Whether in basic or advanced adult education, however, the starting point — indeed the curriculum — are the issues which most affect the learners' daily lives and 'generate' discussion. Within Freire's general approach, in the attempt to encourage participation and dialogue, a whole series of 'participatory techniques' have evolved which help learners step back from and analyse objectively their own immediate reality. Within a planned framework of ever-deeper questioning, the use of photographs, role play and drama techniques, for example, have proved particularly exciting (see Arnold and Burke, 1983). While teachers and invited 'experts' have important contributions to make, the aim is to combat dependency on teachers and to collectively 'empower' groups to take control of their own learning in a way which can best strengthen their ability to struggle for change.

The politics of language teaching

The reader may question the relevance of this discussion to the teaching of modern languages (as opposed to, say, politics or economics). Inescapably, however, language teaching too takes place within a cultural, ideological and political framework. In the teaching of languages to adults, liberal and conservative approaches have undoubtedly prevailed and though individual tutors — and coursebooks — may introduce aspects of radicalism into their teaching, at present this lacks the support of anything grandiose enough to call an articulated, radical approach.

At least until recently, it is the values of liberal education which have dominated adult language courses run by providers such as universities and community education. Curriculums have aimed to meet the needs of individual students, most of whom are motivated by intrinsic interest in the culture and country(ies) where the language is spoken. Good institutions have tried to promote a progressive, student-centred methodology, develop independent learning, provide varied training opportunities for tutors, attempt to put students at ease and even negotiate parts of the curriculum. This falls clearly within the liberal, humanist tradition as espoused by educational theorists such as Malcolm

Knowles and Carl Rogers. CILT's excellent *The adult language learner* also comes under this mantle, with specific reference made to Rogers early on (Arthur and Hurd, 1992, 20). This tradition does not exclude adult learners with a vocational interest, however: the good 'liberal' adult educator always seeks to meet students' needs, vocationalism being no exception.

This author is a defender of the liberal tradition, in so far as it goes. It is commendable that education is valued for its own sake — not simply as a means to an economic end — and for its contribution towards improving the quality of life; in the case of languages, it is good that society recognises the humanistic value of closer cultural affinity with international neighbours. From a radical perspective, however, it has limitations in that, fundamentally, it does not challenge learners to make the world a better place. In trying to service the needs of individuals, 'liberal' language teaching can easily end up helping confirm conservative views.

The conservative approach to teaching languages is most clearly manifest in the whole area of 'languages for business'. 'Business' is presumed to be something positive and courses are designed to help students slot into a business environment in another language (and culture). The raison d'être of business, of course, is to make profit and whether languages for business targets owners, managers or workers, ultimately the aim is to help in the greater accumulation of profit for owners or shareholders. Outwith the explicit focus on business, there is also a plethora of language qualifications designed specifically to serve the needs of employers. The Chamber of Commerce's FLIC and FLAW, NVQs, the work of the Languages Lead Body in England and Wales, for example, would all come into this category.

Education which aims to meet the needs and interests of employers is conservative. If carried out in the belief that what is good for employers is good for society as a whole, then this is explicitly 'Conservatism'. If it is believed that employers have the same right as everyone else to have their needs met, then though ostensibly liberal, its results too are conservative: language teaching which acquiesces in and does not challenge, for example, a multi-national company's right to exploit cheap labour in Third World countries, expropriate large profits, sell weapons of destruction or engage in environmentally damaging economic activity is not 'politically neutral', to quote Freire, but 'sides with the oppressors', even if by default.

This article does not propose that the language needs of employers and business should be ignored. What is proposed is that there ought to be more explicit recognition of the political bias underpinning any attempt to service these needs uncritically. On submitting an article to a mainstream languages journal, for example, this author experienced rejection on the grounds that the article was considered 'overtly political' — which it was — though the same journal saw nothing wrong with its regular features on 'languages for business'. It is perfectly legitimate that there are different views regarding politics and language teaching: the task is not to pretend that they do not exist but to make them explicit — to make the 'covert' 'overt' — so that all language teachers, regardless of political persuasion, have a heightened awareness of the extra-linguistic aspects of their work.

Language teaching with a social purpose

If language teachers adopt a radical perspective and accept Freire's rejection of 'neutrality' — choosing to side with the oppressed, as opposed to oppressors — the next task is to consider how this might be translated into classroom practice. Here, Freire's ideas on literacy have some relevance. Even at the most basic level, since language does not exist independently of ideas and culture, while engaging with the functions, syntax and structure of another language, students can be simultaneously challenged to 'read the world'. Given the cultural focus on another country, moreover, the study of a second language is a useful context in which to look at the international aspects of poverty and oppression, an important issue in times of increasing economic and cultural globalisation. With regard to course content, there are three main areas, I believe, in which language teaching can make a contribution towards progressive education.

The first of these is to ensure that in the process of acquiring language skills, students are acquainted with the world seen from the perspective of those considered 'oppressed' in the areas where the language is spoken. Teaching French, for example, it is important not to present France simply as a country of white, middle-class, nuclear families (though there is nothing wrong in belonging to any of these categories). A language course could bring alive the concerns of the economically poorest in France, whether unemployed or badly-paid workers, for example, or ethnic minority groups such as Moroccans or Senegalese suffering problems of racism. The same would apply to any language or country.

But many European languages are also spoken in parts of the 'third world'. In the UK, research indicates a predominance of negative images of people from the 'third world', mainly due to an imperial past and the effect of the media: drought, famine, mud huts, flies on faces, natural disasters, passive victims dependent on 'first world' charity (see Meakin, 1996). Even from the beginning, at the stage of introducing different native speakers — saying who they are and where they live, describing their daily routines etc — a language course can confront these stereotypes and give voice to those who suffer the worst of oppressions. When people from Haiti, Burkina Faso, Brazil or Guatemala, for example, are allowed to tell their own stories, they challenge the image of passive victim and provide a very different slant (from 'natural disasters') on the causes of poverty. As cultural background, even a critical examination of why European languages are spoken around the globe in the first place raises important questions about imperialism, slavery, expropriation of wealth and continued 'first world' dominance, to name a few. Some coursebooks may already contain material of this nature but the interested teacher can improve on this, actively seek out the voice of the 'oppressed' and build up his/her own bank of authentic materials, usefully categorised for lingusitic ability.

Maintaining the focus on the 'third world', as well as allowing the oppressed to speak for themselves it is possible to engage openly in 'Development Education' through the medium of the language being studied. Strongly supported by agencies such as Oxfam, Christian Aid, CAFOD and SCIAF, Development Education encourages students to explore and discuss the causes of world poverty, especially in relation to first world-third world connections. Kane shows how even a basic language lesson on food can introduce this extra dimension: at a supermarket checkout, on seeing a newspaper headline on famine, a customer asks why people in the 'third world' often go hungry. In pointing out that his basket contains coffee from Ethiopia, tea from Sri Lanka, bananas from Jamaica and flowers from Kenya, for example, the cashier shows how land in the 'third world' can be devoted to the needs of richer countries as opposed to those of the poorest. The field of Development Education has produced a plethora of discussion-based activities — accompanied by relevant, accessible information on the issues concerned — many of which can be adapted to a foreign language classroom. These range from analysing photographs and cartoons, ranking exercises, role play and drama, to full-blown simulation games: they encourage students to consider who makes decisions and who benefits from change and they cover topics as wide apart as the arms trade, the control of food production and debates about population. Teachers can have access to these resources either by visiting a Development Education Centre or ordering an education catalogue from one of the organisations mentioned (an Oxfam Education Catalogue, for example, sells resources from a number of agencies; it also provides addresses of DECs).

Language teachers must be selective, of course, about which development education activity can be adapted to which particular class: linguistically, some activities are simple while others are complex; some are easily adaptable, others may require significant preparation. Importantly, there are many European organisations involved in Development Education which use similar activities in their own countries (see Kirby B, 1994) and these are a useful source of authentic, tailor-made resources.

The second area is that in both the receptive and productive stages of language learning, students can engage in discussing social issues pertaining to their own society as well as that of others. Again, this can be done from an early stage and need not be postponed till language skills are highly developed. In their video showing comic sketches for beginners in Spanish, for example, Kane and Morrison (1993) have a section on 'talking politics' though the main linguistic focus is simply the first person plural of regular verbs in the present tense. In the French Level Two course at Glasgow University's Department of Adult and Continuing Education, to introduce past tenses, one dialogue fictitiously takes place at the pearly gates between the Christian figure of St Peter and a certain Guy Fawkes the Second who wishes to enter the kingdom of heaven. St Peter learns that like his ancestor before him, Guy Fawkes the Second has tried to blow up the British parliament. Unlike the previous occasion, his attempt was successful though, unfortunately, he also killed himself in the process. St Peter is horrified at such brutality but when Guy Fawkes explains what politicians have done to the most vulnerable in society (in past years, issues highlighted have been the poll tax and the closure of Ravenscraig, for example; next year it is likely to be attacks on single parents and the disabled) he understands that something is seriously wrong. At the end, in the role of angels, the class decides whether he enters heaven or not. Tongue-in-cheek, the dialogue attempts to introduce serious issues in an entertaining way and works particularly well when tutors act out the dialogue in front of the class (see Kane, 1995 for a fuller explanation). Follow-up work challenges students to think about the issues and provides linguistic models to help them express their opinions. Importantly, students also have the option not to discuss the issues, a useful approach being to provide, for example, a list of open-ended questions of which students select ten to answer, according to their interests: some questions deal with the serious issues and some do not. The important thing is that the issues are being raised in the classroom and challenge the students to think. Though education cannot be neutral, equally, any attempt to force-feed a particular viewpoint would be in the worst tradition of 'banking' education as described by Freire: people must come to their own conclusions and dogmatic teaching, even from a progressive viewpoint, is essentially reactionary in that people are treated as 'objects' rather than 'subjects'.

When students see from example that even at a basic level it is possible to engage with important issues and not simply talk about hotels, directions or the post office — important as these functions are — it opens the door for students themselves to set the agenda and bring up challenging issues which they themselves consider important. I normally divide students into groups of four and ask them to write a short play over the last few weeks of term and perform it in the last class. Every year, without fail, some groups choose to tackle serious issues, albeit with a certain amount of humour. One year, for example, after only eighteen hours of learning Spanish, one group, suitably attired, acted out the life of a South African orange and its journey to Scotland (in the days of apartheid) and finished off by asking students to support the boycott. On another occasion a group delivered a weather forecast which doubled as political satire. Students were able to enjoy themselves, practice what they had learned but be challenged to think — even to take action — at the same time.

As previously acknowledged, it is important for radical education that in any discussion of social issues, students also consider possible action for change. At this point it would be good to introduce the work of international solidarity organisations (such as Amnesty International or the Central American Committee for Human Rights, for example) or campaigning organisations indigenous to the countries where the language is spoken. If the issues under discussion are domestic, the same considerations apply.

While the first two areas relate to the content of teaching, the third focuses on methodology and the language teacher new to either development or 'Freirian' education could be in for a pleasant surprise. Since both these fields attempt to promote dialogue and discussion in an interesting, participatory manner, they have produced a plethora of activities, games and 'participatory techniques' specifically designed for the purpose. Fortuitously, however, many of these double as ideal examples of 'communicative language activities'. I once worked as a development education worker for Oxfam while teaching a Spanish class in the evening. Some of my best activities in the language class were really adaptations of materials from development education: language teachers following the 'Communicative Approach' would find a wealth of inspiration here, even if, ironically, they were not committed to education for change! To mention a few, Oxfam's video on Africa and Scotland has an unusual, though Freirian, way of challenging stereotypes of Africa by showing the opposite of what is expected: good things, only, about Africa and bad things about Scotland. It is designed to provoke discussion, debate and critical thinking rather than to preach. Christian Aid's 'Globingo' is a superb, flexible, ready-made language exercise, easily adaptable to all levels and provides students with a welcome opportunity to walk around the classroom while simultaneously learning about global interdependence. Augusto Boal's book on 'Games for Actors and Non-Actors' is an inspiration to anyone interested in role play and introduces novel ideas for using drama in social education.

Finally, it is important to be realistic and consider also the limitations on language teaching's contribution to social change. As regards teachers, the demands are greater than normal: language skills alone are insufficient and while there is no need for a degree in global economics, a basic knowledge of development issues would be helpful (as could be acquired from books such as Regan C, 1996; Bissio R, 1997 or Menchu R, 1991). A major weakness is that as yet there is no organised body to bring progressive language teachers together: radical teaching can be an isolated, individualistic activity and would gain strength from organisation and sharing of practice. As regards students, research tends to show that education for change is most effective when a group is already organised around a particular social issue and then looks for educational support for their struggle (e.g. Freire, 1978): a language class, on the other hand, is a group of different individuals who just happen to have been thrown together. In the most optimistic scenario, discussing issues and the possibilities for action may give birth to an interested, organised group of campaigners. A more realistic outcome, however, would be that interested individuals might go on to join other campaigning groups which are already established. A typical adult language class is also predominantly middle-class and arguably less inclined to sympathise with a political perspective giving priority of place to the interests of a different social class. In Freirian language, the 'generative' issues will differ from those of the 'oppressed' (though the meaning of 'oppressed' requires elaboration). While this is true, the exercise remains worthwhile firstly, because it is at least arguable that a better society for the poor is a better society for all and, secondly, because committed, progressive members of the middle class have always had an important role to play in any movement for social change. Perhaps the key question is not where people come from but whose side they are on.

Much remains to be done, then, if language teaching is to play a significant role within radical, adult education. In the drive towards accreditation, however, the more immediate problem could simply be holding on to what is already achievable. While liberal adult education has limitations, it has at least allowed language teachers the option of raising social issues in the classroom. In the current climate it is this option, first and foremost, which has to be safeguarded. The next section explores the politics of accreditation and describes one attempt to ensure that the option survives.

Accreditation

If for no other reason than the need to continue to attract government subsidy, university departments of adult education are now in the business of formally accrediting their courses, languages being no exception. While there was initial debate (Barr, 1996) as to whether accreditation was an attack on liberal adult education or its 'coming of age', it is clear that discussion of accreditation of language courses has moved on and is now concerned with which particular scheme to adopt.

However, the design (or even existence) of a scheme is not simply an abstract, technical matter for it relates to our underlying conception of the purpose of education. (It should be noted that this author has no fundamental opposition to accreditation or assessment per se: key questions, however, are what purpose and whose interests do they serve?). It is of concern that in the understandable desire to adapt to the new reality and accentuate the positive, adult educators may turn their backs on more fundamental educational (and political) issues. Let us at least carry out our discussion of accreditation within the framework of a wider vision for education — not as an isolated, technical issue — and with openness, honesty and a critical awareness of why we do what we do.

However implicit, two themes run through the papers produced by the Scottish Higher Education Funding Council (and its equivalent in England and Wales) regarding the push for accreditation. One is that this will better meet the demands of the market economy, an argument which, though highly suspect even in its own terms (Barr, 1996), lies squarely within the camp of conservative education. A second is that it simplifies the administrative tasks of the funding organisations (albeit with some attempt to equate the latter with the needs of learners). Midst all the arguments for and against accreditation, then, it is crucial not to forget that the government's pressure for the accreditation of liberal adult education has no solid foundation on educational grounds (though it sometimes appears as part of the project to widen access to Higher Education, an admirable aim in its own right but a separate consideration). There was no prior research into the needs of continuing education students to indicate a desirability for the change; there was no attempt to address the arguments against accreditation; scant attention has been paid to the financial and bureaucratic consequences of implementing the changes. The motivation has been a mixture of conservative educational conviction and bureaucratic convenience.

From a radical, or even liberal, approach to language teaching, while accreditation is apparently here to stay, there are two parallel areas, I believe, in which its conservative thrust can be challenged. The first regards the general area of ideological debate: while the decisions of funding bodies cannot be ignored, they should not be allowed to put a lid on discussion of fundamental issues. The benefits of non-accredited education can still be defended, the flimsy grounds on which the funding councils' arguments are based can be exposed and the politically conservative nature of the whole exercise made explicit. Someday the climate will change, new opportunities may arise and it is important that alternative visions of adult education continue to argue their corner.

The second area concerns the more practical exercise of designing or selecting an assessment scheme which best reflects a fundamentally liberal (or even radical) educational philosophy. Entwhistle's research

(1992) in this area is enlightening. In studying how best to promote what he calls 'deep' as opposed to 'surface' learning, he showed that even when the aims, objectives and methodology of a course promoted 'deep' learning, if methods of assessment tested 'surface' learning then this is what had greatest impact on how and what students learned. For those designing systems of accreditation for continuing education, the lesson is to be aware that regardless of how lofty the aims and objectives, assessment could be a 'tail wagging a dog'.

In Glasgow University's Department of Adult and Continuing Education — where there are currently some 1,100 adults enrolled in seventy three language courses — there has been student support for the liberal tradition and strong reaction against accreditation. In designing our system we have conducted research at all stages both with the students and the 55 part-time tutors employed by the department. Space prevents a detailed study of these findings but the following highlights what are considered the main features in our attempt to produce a system of accreditation posing least threat to the traditions of liberal adult education.

- In view of the dangers inherent in Entwhistle's findings it is important that neither existing models of assessment nor administrative convenience becomes the driving force behind a system's design. Accordingly, the first step is to devise a course appropriate to the learners; the second step is then to work out a system of accreditation which least detracts from the original course design. The 'dog should wag the tail'.

- It is better to think in terms of assessment being formative (helping learners improve) rather than summative (helping measure precise levels of competence). Summative assessment — giving students grades, for example — carries the danger of bringing an ethos of competition into the classroom. While students are given extensive 'formative' feedback on individual performance, we have opted to award a simple 'pass' or 'not yet passed' at the end of the year.

- It is not helpful to discourage adults by brandishing them as failures, especially slower learners, and most people in continuing education suffer severe pressures on their time. Accordingly, we have resisted the pressure to aim for high levels of credit which could make courses either too difficult or too demanding. Our pass level is based on the minimum satisfactory competence we would expect from a student who attends the course and does some but not much work in between. This is reflected in the credit awarded (only 10 SCOTCAT points per 40-hour course). It is not a fast-track route to a degree — for that students must look elsewhere — but it is based on the needs of adults in continuing education.

- Only a sample of students' work should require formal assessment: the constant gripe of students and tutors in vocational schemes (such as SCOTVEC, for example), is that too much time is wasted on assessing everything, not enough is spent on learning. Our students are assessed four times in the year with two assessments normally related to listening/speaking and two to reading/writing.

- There should be enough flexibility in the Intended Learning Outcomes (ILOs) to allow some negotiation of the curriculum.

- It is not necessary to assess all students in exactly the same ILO. A list of possible ILOs for each assessment means that the class can move ahead at a normal pace with a few students being assessed each week. Appendix 1, p115, gives an example of our assessment scheme for a typical course.

- Tutors and students can negotiate the most appropriate way to carry out assessment. It can be done a) as a normal classroom activity without students being told it is an assessment b) with a few students each week, where students have time to prepare beforehand or even c) with all students being assessed in the same activity on the same night.

- Rather than a bolted-on extra for ambitious students, we have tried to make assessment as non-threatening as possible and relevant to everyone. Accordingly, while we defend students' right not to be assessed, we ask them to opt out rather than to opt in. In the long run, we suspect that funding for adult education may be tied to completion rates: from the very start we would like to establish that our system of accreditation has been designed with the needs of all students in mind.

It is hoped that this approach will protect the best of liberal adult education. Student and tutor attitudes are being monitored and while of those students who have dropped out of courses, few cited 'assessment' as the problem, we cannot be sure it did not play a part (equally, where assessment was quoted, we are not convinced this was the real problem either). Our tutors continue to have varying opinions on the effects of accreditation. There are many variables involved in the analysis, however (such as the attitude and ability of tutors, the amount and quality of training provided, the previous experience of learners), and a proper evaluation of the impact of assessment may take some time to emerge. As long as there is a degree of 'liberalism' — as opposed to a centralised, tightly-controlled set of demands — then radical education can still take place alongside the teaching of language skills.

Conclusion

On its own, education will not change the world: to argue otherwise is, in every sense, idealistic. It can play a part in bringing about change, however, though its precise contribution is notoriously difficult to measure. Albeit with limitations, language teaching too has much to offer the area of education for social change. It is also possible to resist the conservative thrust behind accreditation and continue to offer a liberal adult education which allows a more radical approach to persist. To learn from the wider world of education for change, however, strength is acquired through organisation: perhaps it is time to set up a forum for language teachers committed to social change. This would help with the sharing of ideas, would raise the profile of the issues and could serve as an alternative point of reference to the 'languages-for-business' school of thought: this author would be happy to hear from anyone interested in joining such a venture.

Bibliography

Arnold R and B Burke, *A popular education handbook* (Canada: CUSO and OISE Ontario, 1983)

Arthur L and S Hurd, *The adult language learner* (CILT, 1992)

Barr J, 'The SHEFC Review of Continuing Education' in *International Journal of Lifelong Education* (Vol 15, No. 6 Nov–Dec 1996)

Bissio R (ed), *The world guide* (New Internationalist Publications, 1997)

Boal A, *Games for actors and non-actors* (Routledge, 1992)

Entwhistle N, S Thompson and H Tait, *Guidelines for promoting effective learning in Higher Education* (Centre for Research on Learning and Instruction, 1992)

Freire P, *Pedagogy of the oppressed* (Penguin, 1972)

Freire P, 'Education, liberation and the Church' in *Study Encounter* (Vol 9, No. 1, 1973)

Freire P, *Pedagogy in process* (London Writers and Readers Publishing Co-operative, 1978)

Gramsci A, *Selections from the prison notebooks* (Lawrence and Wishart, 1971)

Herman E S and N Chomsky, *Manufacturing consent: the political economy of the mass media* (Vintage, 1994)

Kane L, 'Modern languages and development education' in *World Studies Journal* (Vol 7, No. 2 1989)

Kane L, 'Making a drama out of a crisis' in *Language Learning Journal* (No. 11, March 1995)

Kane L and E Morrison, *Hablando en Broma* (University of Glasgow, 1993)

Kirby B (ed), *Education for change: grassroots development education in Europe* (Development Education Association, 1994)

Knowles M S, *Modern practice of adult education: from pedagogy to andragogy* (USA: Association Press, 1980)

Mackie R (ed), *Literacy and revolution: the pedagogy of Paulo Freire* (Pluto, 1980)

Mayo M and J Thompson (eds), *Adult learning, critical intelligence and social change* (NIACE, 1995)

Meakin C B, *Guidelines for global issues in technology* (Intermediate Technology, 1996)

Menchu R, *I Rigoberta Menchú* (Verso, 1991)

Rattansi A and D Reeder (eds), *Rethinking radical education: essays in honour of Brian Simon* (Lawrence & Wishart, 1992)

Regan C (ed), *75:25 development in an increasingly unequal world* (Birmingham DEC, 1996)

Rogers C R, *Freedom to learn* (USA: Merrill, 1994)

Rowntree foundation inquiry into income and wealth (Rowntree Froundation, 1995)

United Nations Human Development Report (United Nations, 1997)

Westwood S, 'When class became community: radicalism in adult education' in Rathansi A and D Reeder, *Rethinking radical education: essays in honour of Brian Simon* (Lawrence & Wishard, 1992)

Student attitudes to learning, assessment and accreditation

2

Fran Beaton, Goldsmiths College

This paper looks at adult education students' perception of accreditation and the effect this has on the teaching and learning of MFLs in a single institution. This is in the context of a programme area entirely funded by FEFC and HEFCE and therefore required to offer students the opportunity for accreditation. Since the original writing of the paper (1997) it has become explicit that accreditation is not only a desirable outcome of courses, but that programme outcome will be monitored within that context. External funding will depend to a much greater extent than before on whether students actually **participate** in assessment procedures, rather than simply on the institutional provision of these.

This paper examines three aspects of this question. It will compare the motivation and attitude of students attending a programme of study of English as a Foreign Language to those attending a programme of study in Modern Foreign Languages. It will examine the tensions which can arise between formal requirements, tutor perception and students' own interests and needs. It will then describe a system of accreditation and the development of a more user-friendly approach to enable students to achieve their personal learning goals.

Motivating the adult learner

For the adult learner there are several considerations affecting the approach to study. These include the nature and purpose of study itself; the learner's perception of the role of the student and the tutor in identifying and achieving short- or long-term goals; the individual's learning style, and their level of strategic competence; and finally the extent to which the learner regards the activities of the student group as compatible with his or her aims. This embraces factors such as tutor selection of topics, materials and activities, the comparative emphasis on fluency and accuracy and approaches to the teaching of, for example, grammar. Affective factors, significant whether generated by the adult learner's experience outside or within the classroom, further play a part in determining how and whether motivation is sustained and outcomes achieved.

Cultural attitudes to the purpose of adult education

Rogers (1992:1) identified the purpose of adult education in the West as being traditionally characterised by '*a desire for individual growth . . . an essentially voluntary process, offered to all and taken up by relatively few*'. He contrasts this with the attitude in many developing countries, where Adult education is perceived as a driving force for realising nationally identified, quantifiable goals, be they basic literacy targets or developing a highly trained labour force. In the latter case it is assumed that all will participate as good citizens and that personal growth is a secondary consideration. Rogers identifies three principal and overlapping roles which characterise adult life experiences as learners. These are the **occupational,** the **social** and the **attitudinal**, and each has a profound influence on the adult learner's view of their continuing learning, and by extension on how a learner quantifies and perceives the outcomes of this. Rogers argues that these three strands are vital for each individual, but also that in the Western world in the 1990s there is a prevalent climate in which holistic personal development is allied to occupational development, including adjustment to social change. His claim that these two concepts of learning had been regarded as mutually exclusive (and this is in the early 1990s) and were increasingly regarded as complementary is one which has still greater resonance in the current climate. Personal development can only take place if it '*calls from the people a range of decisions and actions (which) make the change effective*' (Rogers, 1992: 3). In other words, the adult learner needs to feel that their participation in learning is grounded in their own experience and current state, and acknowledges the value of the learner's own attitudes, needs, resources and aspirations.

For adult learners of languages these factors are further intensified by the nature of language itself. While language is composed of features such as grammar, lexis, register (and learners will rightly anticipate that any language instruction will include these as part of skills development), each learner will have a personal concept of how they wish to use the language. This concept is likely to be based on the learner's sociolinguistic experience in L1, and while most learners of a foreign language will not expect to reach a native-speaker degree of competence, they may well expect to be offered increasingly more cognitively challenging situations within which they can function as performers in L2. This performance may be in personal or professional, private or public settings, and the challenge in many teaching situations is the breadth of performance expectations which different learners may bring. In addition, the differing notions of language proficiency postulated by Stern (1991) including as they do the concepts of formal, semantic and strategic mastery as components in communicative competence may not be ones with which students are explicitly familiar; however many learners will have a concept of these elements as applied to L1 and C1 interactions and will expect these to be features of their L2 experience. The next question is to consider what learners expect that experience to include. *'Language teaching practice has demonstrated an increasing concern with the process of learning . . . and is a logical outcome of teachers' concern that learners should be able to assume responsibility for that learning (while teachers may be) fearful of an* "anarchy of expectations" *'* (Bloor and Bloor in Edge and Richards, 1993: 65).

Given the breadth of age and experience of adult learners of foreign languages, it is not surprising that in any given classroom today there will be learners who have previously experienced a number of different teaching styles. In terms of the teaching of modern languages, these will have been dictated not only by the specific teaching milieu but also by prevailing methodological trends and assumptions about how learning is achieved. The adult learner is therefore likely to have some sort of model of what he or she regards as effective teaching, and will have that in mind when assessing subsequent teaching/learning experiences. We evaluate new experiences, at least initially, in the light of previous experiences, whether positive or negative. For students this may take the form of expressing an anxiety about a particular area of language or types of interaction ('Can we do more grammar?' 'I don't like listening to other people's mistakes!'), which may be the fruits of earlier classroom contact.

Testing and lifelong learning

If the educational debate has generated discussion about the nature of learning and tutors' and students' role in the learning process, the heat of that debate has been further intensified by attempts to define the relationship of teaching and testing.

In adult education, as in schools, the concept of 'teaching to the test' is one which has been debated. In the field of language testing there are general and specific criteria, such as the validity (both of content and construct) and reliability of the test, the likely effect of the test on the learner; and arising from that, the perceived relationship of the test content to what has been taught or learned. If the learner regards the business of testing as threatening, irrelevant or beyond their experience, then he or she is unlikely to welcome a situation in which it is covertly or overtly enforced; and if we accept that adults are autonomous participants in the process of lifelong learning, then we have to respect this position.

As adult educators, we are thus in a position where institutionally there are financial incentives if we can demonstrate positive student outcomes on accredited courses. This can even be more discouragingly presented as disincentives if these outcomes are non-quantifiable, and is difficult to reconcile this with the notion that learning is a richly varied and ongoing phenomenon. In addition as linguists we know that language proficiency is a dynamic process, lending itself to a structured process within a creative framework which may not be shared by all learners. In other words, in the same beginners class there may be learners who are embarking on their second foreign language and intend to study it to a comparably high level, and learners who are returning to study after a number of years who wish to learn enough language to get by in the country. The teaching demands are already considerable; when the tutor is faced with preparing such diverse students for a test then these demands multiply.

The second part of this paper will describe an attempt to deal with these issues in the context of one continuing education department. It will compare the aspirations and experience of students on an English language programme of study and those attending modern languages classes, and evaluate the appropriacy and effectiveness of the accreditation scheme for these target groups. Finally it will look at future developments and adjustments in the process to meet the needs of our learners and move towards a broader takeup of the accreditation paths offered.

Background to the programme

The part-time languages programme includes ten modern languages. Four of these (French, German, Italian and Spanish) cater for all levels of student from beginner (Level 1) to very advanced (Level 6). The remaining languages (Arabic, Chinese, Irish, Japanese, Portuguese and Russian) are offered up to Level 3. In the 1996/97 session there were some 450 students, ranging in age from 25 to over 65, attending modern languages classes at various levels, for between 60–120 hours per year.

Whatever the amount of contact time, students are fitting in their learning around all manner of other commitments; as Lore Arthur has pointed out *'anyone who has ever attempted to (attend adult education classes) will know just how much courage, sacrifice and sheer determination is required'* (Hawkins, 1996:53). Typically, in the course of an academic year, student dropout is in the region of 20%, with the most frequently cited reason being pressure of work or changing family circumstances.

Modern foreign languages students

Analysis of students' records revealed that the majority (nearly 80%) had studied for professional qualifications at post-compulsory level, and nearly a quarter had studied a foreign language at university level. A 'snapshot' survey conducted in February 1997 further produced the information that nearly 60% of students were attending classes to study their second foreign language, although very few of these were encouraged by their families or employers to do so. It was also rare for students to report that their language learning was implicitly or explicitly linked to career development. The notable exception to this were ten out of fifteen students in a Japanese class, all of whom were working in settings where a knowledge of Japanese, however basic, was seen as a positive professional advantage.

English for speakers of other languages

By contrast, the English programme (offered from Levels 2–5) had 350 students attending, predominantly aged between 18 and 25 and studying for between 120–180 hours per year. Many of these were short-term residents here i.e. recent school leavers, spending a gap year in the UK, intending to return to their own country within twelve months to embark on further training or enter higher education. At the time in question over 80% of the EFL students stated that they regarded examination success as a *sine qua non* of the course, and had a clear perception of the future value of examination success in terms of access to employment or higher education. The examination itself consists of five components, of which sample details of the requirements for the intermediate level examination appear on pp30–31.

It is striking that what many languages teachers and learners would regard as a key feature for students at this level (interpersonal oral skills) has only been a component of this test for the last three years.

Framework for guidance and advice

Irrespective of language, all would-be students are interviewed by the subject co-ordinator or a language specialist. This interview assesses a student's previous learning experience, their degree of contact with the language — whether formal or informal — their current level of oral proficiency and their immediate or long-term learning goal. All students are given advice about the learning resources available to them as students of the college, and the opportunity for accreditation is raised at the same time.

FIRST CERTIFICATE IN ENGLISH
(FCE – Cambridge Level 3)

The First Certificate Examination is at Level 3 in the Cambridge five level system. It tests general competence in English and is often taken after approximately 500 to 600 hours of study.

FCE has widespread recognition in commerce and industry, e.g. for public contact or secretarial work in banking, airlines, catering, etc. and in individual university faculties, colleges and other institutions.

EXAMINATION CONTENT

Paper 1	**Reading** (1 hour and 15 minutes)

This paper consists of 35 questions (multiple matching, multiple choice, gapped text) on four texts, one of which may be a multi-text.

The paper is designed to test understanding of gist, main points, detail, text structure, specific information or the deduction of meaning.

This paper carries 40 marks.

Paper 2	**Writing** (1 hour and 30 minutes)

In this paper candidates are required to complete two writing tasks of approximately 120-180 words each.

Part 1: a compulsory letter writing task based on reading input.

Part 2: one task selected from a choice of four involving the production of one of the following text types: an article, a report, a letter, a composition task or a task on a prescribed background reading text.

One or more of the following texts may be read as background preparation for optional tasks in Paper 2:

Charles Dickens, *Great expectations* (Longman Bridge/Longman Fiction)*

Edgar Alan Poe, *Tales of mystery and imagination* (Longman Fiction)

Oxford Bookworm Collections, *Crime never pays* (OUP)*

Daphne du Maurier, *Rebecca* (Longman Fiction)*

Ernest Hemingway, *The old man and the sea* (any edition)

* set also in 1997

The paper tests range of vocabulary and structure; accuracy of vocabulary, structure, spelling and punctuation; appropriacy; organisation and cohesion; task achievement.

This paper carries 40 marks.

| **Paper 3** | **Use of English** (1 hour and 15 minutes) |

This paper consists of 65 questions in five compulsory tasks; multiple choice cloze, open cloze, 'key' word transformations, error correction, word formation.

This paper is designed to test active control of the grammar and vocabulary of the language.

This paper carries 40 marks.

| **Paper 4** | **Listening** (approximately 40 minutes) |

This paper consists of 30 questions (multiple choice, note taking or blank filling, multiple matching, selection from two or three possible answers) in four parts. Each part contains recorded text or texts of a range of types. The paper is designed to test understanding of gist, main points, detail or specific information or the deduction of meaning.

This paper carries 40 marks.

| **Paper 5** | **Speaking** (approximately 14 minutes) |

Paper 5 in its standard format is conducted in pairs with two examiners. The interaction is based on visual and oral prompts. Candidates are required to give and exchange information and opinions through a range of task types (e.g. conversation, planning, problem solving, discussion).

If a centre has an uneven number of candidates, the last pair of candidates in a session should form a group of three to incorporate the extra candidate.

NB: This group of three formats may only be used to deal with uneven numbers, unexpected absence of candidates, illness, etc. It is not an option that may be selected in normal circumstances where there is an even number of candidates at a session.

There is a one candidate to one examiner format which may be used in exceptional circumstances provided that prior approval has been given in writing by UCLES. Such approval must be sought by the centre before any entries are accepted.

This paper is designed to test use of grammar, use of vocabulary, pronunciation, interactive communication and task achievement.

This paper carries 40 marks.

NB1: Background reading texts are not available for optional tasks in Paper 5.
NB2: Optional papers are not available.

Results

Certificates are awarded in three passing grades A, B and C on the aggregate of marks gained in the five compulsory papers indicated above, with results also in three failing grades D, E and U (unclassified). Results slips (on which see p4) for candidates in the passing grades A, B and C contain information about their overall grade and, where appropriate, about the papers in which these candidates achieved a high level of performance. Results slips for candidates in the failing grades D and E (but not U) contain information about their overall grades and, where appropriate, about the papers in which there was a particularly weak level of performance.

Differing perceptions of English language and MFL students

It is at this point that marked differences in perception and motivation begin to emerge. For many students joining the English programme, their stated motivation was almost entirely instrumental and directed at a specific goal, that is the successful passing of an examination. Many were used to directed learning along specific pathways, and they were disinclined to question the means by which this would be achieved, or their role in the process. The qualification in question (awarded by the University of Cambridge) is internationally widely recognised; secondly, English language competence is regarded as a key skill in many professional, academic and service settings. Many students therefore have a clear perception that English language qualifications will be of practical value at some point in the immediate or imaginable future. In total, 90% of students on course took examinations; of these 80% passed, with a further 15% passing at a subsequent sitting.

This is in marked contrast to the motivation and backgrounds of learners of modern foreign languages. In the previously mentioned 'snapshot' survey, students typically reported that they had studied and been examined at a high level already, either in languages or in the course of gaining other professional qualifications. These students regarded their current language studies as being of intrinsic long-term interest rather than subject to the post-compulsory or professional education they had already undergone. Interestingly, however, there were further comments that the fact of offering accreditation made it more likely in the learners' eyes that teaching would be structured, organised and effective and this was perceived as a real incentive to study. Whatever the truth of this, the perception was there, and is compatible with another frequent student comment, namely that a university continuing education department is perceived as offering a rigorous approach to teaching and learning. For tutors on the language programme, many of whom had considerable teaching experience, there was real concern that an assessment-driven programme could run counter to communicative teaching and, particularly at lower levels, lead to high drop-out rates.

Accreditation paths: modern languages

The accreditation paths for modern languages fall into two categories: internally and externally validated. The internally validated scheme (Scheme of Foreign Language Proficiency) is one used with students in the mainstream department and part-time students from elsewhere in the college, including continuing education. It consists of four grades of examination, each subdivided into two levels) from *ab initio* to final year degree standard. These grades are based on the principle that part-time students will complete a level within a grade per academic year, while full-time students, with more classroom contact time, one grade per year. Sample criteria for the first grade appear below.

Scheme of Proficiency: teaching scheme	Grade 1 Preliminary

Aims	• To develop an understanding of everyday language within a limited number of everyday contexts. • To be able to communicate basic needs and requests; to form simple questions and statements in those contexts. • To be able to extract concrete surface information from simple aural and written texts. • To have a basic awareness of cultural norms and registers, e.g. the appropriate use of the personal or polite form.
Grammatical control	• A grasp of the function and use of present tense question, statement and simple negative forms such as to enable communication with a sympathetic native speaker. • An ability to recognise regular past tense forms commonly used in the relevant language and limited productive control of a narrow range of commonly used verbs, e.g. to be, to have, to go. • An understanding of basic word order and simple rules, e.g. those governing adjective agreement.
Lexical features	• A knowledge and competent use of concrete vocabulary in relevant topic areas, e.g. eliciting and giving personal information, asking directions, ordering food and drink, travelling.

Scheme of Proficiency: scheme of assessment	Grade 1 Preliminary

This consists of three components:

1 **Reading comprehension**   Duration 45 minutes   50 marks

Candidates are required to read two passages taken/adapted from an authentic source and to answer questions on these. Most questions will be asked in English and require a short written answer in English. There will also be some multiple choice questions in the foreign language where the candidate will be required to select the correct answer.

At this level no candidate will be expected to write in the foreign language.

2 **Listening comprehension**   Duration 20 minutes   50 marks

Candidates are required to listen to two recordings, either conversations between two people or short extracts of continuous speech. All questions will be asked in English and require a short written answer in that language.

3 **Oral communication**   Duration 10 minutes   50 marks

(a) Candidates are required to take part in a guided role play based on a simple communicative situation. (15 marks)

(b) Candidates are required to take part in a general conversation with the examiner in which they are able to demonstrate an ability to talk about a limited range of everyday topics using present and some simple past tense forms. (35 marks)

Marks will be given separately for each component and an overall mark calculated and expressed as a percentage. The pass mark is 35%.

Scheme of Proficiency: teaching scheme	Grade 1

Aims
- To develop an understanding of everyday language within a range of everyday contexts.
- To be able to elicit and communicate concrete needs, requests, hopes and wishes; to form questions and statements relating to these.
- To be able to extract concrete information from longer simple aural and written texts.
- To be able to convey simple information in the target language in written form.
- To have a developing awareness of and ability to apply cultural norms and registers, e.g. use of personal/polite, formal/informal forms.

Grammatical control
- A good grasp of the function and use of:
  (i) the present form, including uses relating to future meaning;
  (ii)the past tense forms commonly used in the relevant language;
  in questions and statements and simple negative form such as to communicate in a range of everyday contexts.
- An understanding and competent use of the conventions of word order, adjectival agreement.
- An ability to produce coherent written text on an everyday topic.

Lexical features
- A knowledge and competent use of vocabulary in a broader range of topic areas relating to the everyday context, e.g. giving and eliciting personal information, travelling, food and drink.
- A knowledge and competent use of vocabulary relating to issues of general interest, e.g. work or leisure activities.

Scheme of Proficiency: scheme of assessment	Grade 1

1 **Written communication**   Duration 1 hour   50 marks

Candidates are required to answer two questions (each one is allocated 25 marks) in differing formats, e.g. a formal or informal letter, a dialogue between two people, a description of a place, person, situation or event. There should be clear evidence of an ability to use various tenses and grammatically correct languages, albeit in a restricted range.

Each answer should consist of about 100 words.

2 **Reading comprehension**   Duration 45 minutes   50 marks

Candidates are required to read two passages taken/adapted from an authentic source and to answer questions on these. Some questions will be in English and should be answered in English; others will be in the target language and should be answered in full sentences in the target language in students' own words.

3 **Listening comprehension**   Duration 50 minutes   50 marks

Candidates are required to listen to two recordings, either conversations between two people or short extracts of continuous speech. All questions will be asked in English and require a short written answer in that language.

4 **Oral communication**   Duration 10 minutes   50 marks

(a) Role play. Candidates are required to take part in a guided role play based on an everyday situation. (15 marks)

(b) Candidates are required to take part in a general conversation with the examiner in which they are able to demonstrate an ability to talk about a limited range of everyday topics using a variety of tenses. (35 marks)

These criteria are circulated to all tutors, whether in the part-time or the full-time programme; the linguistic content, assessment criteria and task design for each component are set jointly by the mainstream and part-time departments, with tutors from both involved in the setting and marking of the various exam components. These are then moderated at a single examination board, prior to which a representative sample of all students' work is scrutinised by an external examiner.

In other words, a system is in place which is clear, flexible, has transparent criteria for success (and is affordable), of which a very small proportion of part-time students choose to take advantage. The notional advantage, of being able to collect institutional credits which could be used as a route to later full-time study, was not regarded by more than a handful of students as being relevant to their current or future situation.

The externally validated scheme is assessed by the Institute of Linguists, and with the exception of the issue of affordability, many of the apparent advantages associated with the Scheme of Proficiency similarly apply. The quantity of information about the criteria for success at different levels is accessible to students and to tutors, there is an increasing resource bank of material to help students prepare for examination and many of the assessment criteria are similar. Student reaction here is rather different, however. Although the numbers entering for examination are still not great, students were particularly and specifically motivated to join higher level classes to prepare for examination at Intermediate or Final Diploma level. All students reported that this had been a key factor in enrolling on the course, as they were intending to pursue a career in which these high-level language skills were essential. This goal had only emerged after a number of years of part-time study, during which the primary emphasis for the learner had been on developing an understanding and appreciation of the language and the cultures within which it is spoken. Across the whole modern languages programme, fewer than 10% took examinations (chiefly at these higher levels) and 98% passed.

Future planning

There were several clear messages which needed to be built into future planning. If actual or potential students perceive accreditation as largely irrelevant to their personal goals, even when all involved in course design and delivery are themselves persuaded of the transparency of the assessment procedures, how can we reconcile this with the externally driven need to encourage students to enter the process? In planning for the then coming session (97/98), we concluded that for students in the first three levels we should take a more proactive approach in encouraging students to view the assessment process as part of their personal development, giving a sense of intrinsic achievement rather than being a pathway into higher education. This emphasis was reflected in several ways. Firstly, course literature included information about course content and the relationship of this to possible accreditation paths. Secondly, and most critically, as part of staff development we looked at course content, and started to expand a generic resources bank of published and created material. Subject area specialists from the full-time and part-time departments met regularly to exchange materials and ensure that these were accessible to all tutors. Since the full-time department had itself recently undergone a comprehensive reorganisation this was a mutually fruitful exercise. Visiting tutors from both departments were also involved in Inset training events of professional interest. Having established these links, visiting tutors felt more confident about the relationship between what happens in their communicative languages classroom and the exit assessment. This confidence enabled tutors to offer more comprehensive advice to students, delivered with some conviction and based on a more thorough awareness of the materials, methods and processes involved. While it will take some time to see if these adjustments have an impact on students' attitudes to assessment overall, the indications at the time of writing suggest that there has been a gradual movement towards the notion of assessment being viewed as part of personal development. There are more students on programmes than there were at the same time last year; 20% are entering for examination this year. Nearly all reported that the emphasis on the personal sense of achievement, allied to the focused but communicatively oriented work they had been doing in class, had been a key factor in their decision to do so. Future planning will seek to build on this, endeavouring to strike a coherent and achievable balance between externally driven needs and the paramount responsibility we have to offer students genuine access to lifelong learning.

Bibliography

Baker D, *Language testing* (Edward Arnold, 1989)

Edge J and K Richards (eds), *Teachers develop teachers research* (Heinemann, 1993)

Ellis R, 'Communicative strategies and the evaluation of communicative performance' in *English Language Teaching Journal* (OUP, 1984)

Hawkins E, (ed) *30 years of language teaching* (CILT, 1996)

Rogers A, *Adults learning for development* (Cassell, 1992)

Stern H H, *Fundamental concepts of language teaching* (OUP, 1991)

3 | Assessment on a fully accredited Open Language Programme: achieving beneficial backwash in a standardised scheme

Dounia Bissar, University of North London

Assessment suffers from a bad reputation: indeed, it is often perceived in a negative way by students and tutors alike, who associate it with feelings of being overworked, overstressed and other traumas. Yet, at the same time, the benefits of sound evaluation are generally recognised, including its potential to create motivation, develop skills and provide useful feedback on students' performance as well as on the quality of a course. Students themselves can be quite clear about what constitutes good testing practice, relating it to the main concepts of fairness (i.e. clear questions, for which they have been prepared, which are going to be marked objectively, etc) and relevance (i.e. tests directly related to the content and the objectives of the course). To develop a system of assessment that can achieve positive impact, these criteria have to be met. This is even more important when assessment is being introduced into an existing programme (as is presently the case with language courses in university departments of continuing education), because it can be perceived even more as a threat and a burden.

In the area of language teaching, the focus on communicative competence has lead to a new approach to testing, with the aim of finding appropriate ways to measure the ability to communicate. However, as pointed out by Hughes (1989: 6), 'each testing situation is unique and so sets a particular testing problem', and a perfect test cannot be designed. Thus, when developing assessment, the main question to be asked is whether tests are appropriate to measure particular learning outcomes. To this end, criteria have been defined by language testers in recent years, the most elaborated and up to date coming from Bachman and Palmer (1996). Their definition of the qualities necessary for tests to be useful includes reliability, construct validity, authenticity, interactiveness, impact and practicality, all important in various degrees depending on the objectives of particular tests. However, these requirements sometimes conflict with constraints pertaining to the nature of a large programme, mainly the need for standardisation, necessary for consistency across and within languages, material constraints such as an often reduced contact time with the students, and the reliance on part-time tutors (who can only be expected to do a limited amount of extra teaching-related work). Compromises therefore have to be made in order to achieve a balanced system of assessment which can have beneficial backwash on teaching and learning.

The Open Language Programme (OLP) at the University of North London (UNL) provides an illustrative case study for linguists in departments of continuing education. Indeed, even though the context is different in some aspects (for instance, courses are fully accredited and most students take a language as part of their degree), it is nevertheless a new programme, with students from various backgrounds (most of them non-linguist), which has a predominantly vocational purpose, and for which a system of assessment had to be developed taking into account the constraints described above.

The aim of this paper is therefore to present the system of assessment on the OLP at UNL, to propose ways to achieve beneficial backwash in a standardised scheme and to contribute to the debate on assessment and accreditation for languages. The paper will start with theoretical premises which include the context, the purpose of the tests, the subject of assessment and the tests characteristics to consider. The system of assessment will then be presented, followed by an evaluation of that system using a model adapted from Bachman and Palmer's 'plan for the evaluation of usefulness' (1996). Finally, conclusions will be drawn on the suitability of the testing methods presented, their impact on students and tutors, further steps to take and new avenues to explore, and on what a general approach to language testing should be.

Case study: OLP system of assessment at UNL

Context

The OLP offers general language courses with a competence-based communicative syllabus. It is principally aimed at students across the University (about 80%), but also open to staff and the general public. Numbers have increased continuously since it was set up in 1993, with 1,500 students enrolling in 1996/97, 700 in the first semester, 800 in the second. The languages offered are French, Spanish, German, Italian, Russian, Greek and Dutch; Irish is being introduced in 1997/98. These languages are taught at six different levels, corresponding to three stages: beginners, intermediate and advanced, each comprising two modules, which run every semester and last for thirteen weeks, i.e. twelve teaching weeks and one assessment week. The courses combine classroom tuition (one class of 2H45 per week) with guided self-study with especially prepared study packs, using the audio/video and IT facilities available in the Language Centre. Each course is fully accredited within the University's modular scheme, and counts towards the students' degree. Marks obtained are graded according to the University's grading system, with 40% the pass rate.

Thirty-six tutors now work on the programme, the great majority on a part-time basis (as many as 30). To deal with the increasing size of the programme, each language has been assigned a Language Co-ordinator, who is responsible for liaising with the tutors on matters such as course programmes, materials, methodology and, crucially, assessment and boards.

Purpose

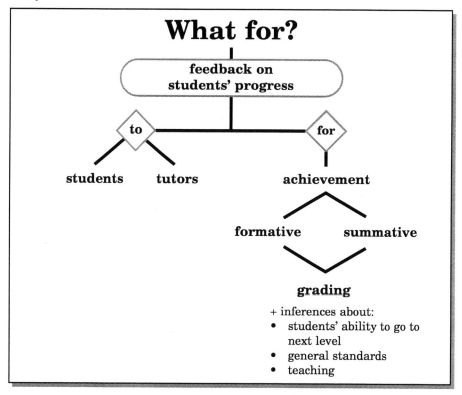

When reflecting upon a system of assessment, the first question that needs to be asked is: what purpose does it serve, why are we assessing the students? Or even, do we need to assess them at all? To encourage students to acquire new language skills or to develop existing ones, all courses on the OLP are fully accredited. Students' performance therefore needs to be measured, i.e. we have to establish how successful they have been in achieving the course objectives, mainly in order to give them a mark. In addition, we need to monitor how well they are progressing through the course. Thus we need a formative as well as a summative type of assessment. Both tutors and students need that feedback, which will also give tutors an indication of how successful their teaching has been. Furthermore, students can benefit from assessment as a learning activity, which helps them to identify better the standards to be reached and the ways to achieve them.

Subject of assessment

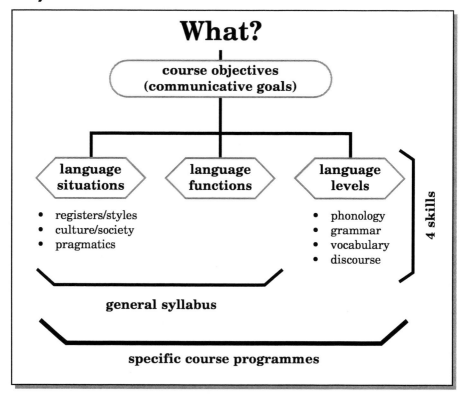

If we are to make valid inferences about our students' language abilities, we need to define what these abilities are. As explained in the section on p39, what needs to be assessed is how well students have achieved the course objectives. These are communicative-based, with the focus initially on understanding and speaking skills, reading and writing increasing in importance during more advanced levels.

Because of the necessity to have minimum parity across the languages at different levels (all modules bear the same credit), individual course programmes are based on a general syllabus common to all languages. This syllabus comprises a list of functions, related to a few suggested main topics or situations, general enough to leave scope for cultural and temporal specification. The levels of phonology, grammar, vocabulary and discourse are of course not included in the syllabus, but outlined in the language-specific course programmes for the six different levels.

Test characteristics

Considering the subject of our assessment and its purpose, we can identify the different characteristics our tests should have in order to be useful. As the main aim is to assess how well students have achieved the course objectives, the tests should represent as much as possible a direct form of testing, i.e. test directly the abilities outlined in the syllabus, rather than test skills underlying these abilities. The tasks included in the tests should be as close as possible to the real life tasks we would expect our students to be able to perform at the end of the course. For the same reason, the tasks and texts submitted should be authentic, reflecting real language use, and the tests should therefore be integrative, i.e. combining a variety of language components (not just grammatical items, for example). If the tasks are to reflect real use of the target language, the tests must be criterion-referenced, in the sense used by Hughes (1989) of tests providing direct information about what students can do with the language. This means tests which measure students' performance in relation to established criteria, with set tasks and standards. In order to ensure parity across and within the languages (especially in the case of multiple-class modules) and to achieve reliability in scoring, we need objective tests, with items determined in advance and well-defined marking criteria. Finally, the need for parity and objectivity requires standardised tests, with standard tasks, performance and marking criteria reflecting the main objectives common to all the languages, while at the same time the design of the tests should leave room for linguistic and cultural specificity.

OLP system of assessment

Overview

Having outlined how we should assess our students, we can now describe how we do assess them within our present system and, afterwards, evaluate whether this matches the theoretical premises.

As explained above, the purpose is to evaluate how well students have achieved the course objectives, and to have feedback on the progress they are making through the course. Thus, for the system of assessment to be valid, it had to include a range of tasks wide enough to cover the different abilities outlined in the course objectives, using the four skills (to a various extent, depending on their importance in the course). Considering that the course only lasts for thirteen weeks, and that, for reasons of flexibility, assessment is test-based and takes place during classroom time, there was a danger of dedicating too much time to testing, at the expense of teaching. For this reason, it would have been difficult to include a form of continuous assessment (to measure students' progress), such as marking some of the work done with the study packs, as it would have been most probably perceived as over-assessment by both students and tutors. Moreover, the unavoidable risk of collaborative work had to be taken into account. Therefore, it was decided to have a system of classroom-based achievement tests which would be administered in two main steps, with a formative evaluation half-way through the course (coursework 1) and a summative evaluation at the end of the course (coursework 2 + coursework 3).

OLP assessment breakdown

	Stage 1	*Stage 2*	*Stage 3*
Coursework 1			
• Cloze test	10%	10%	10%
• Listening comprehension	20%	20%	20%
Coursework 2			
• Written test (letter/message)	20%	20%	20%
• Oral test	50%	40%	40%
	role play (30%) controlled conversation (20%)	role play (2/1) / discussion (2/2) + open conversation	discussion + open conversation
Coursework 3			
• Written assignment	—	10%	10%

Coursework 1

This part of the assessment, which serves to measure the progress students have made since the beginning of the course, takes place during Week 7 class and had to be short to administer so as to leave enough time for teaching activities. Thus a cloze test and a listening comprehension were selected, because while their main focus is on receptive skills (which is an important consideration after only six weeks of the course, especially at beginners' level), they can also provide informative feedback. Both tests are indeed integrative type of tests, and can be constructed to combine the various language elements covered in the first half of the course. Moreover, they are short to administer and straightforward to mark and to correct afterwards with the students.

The cloze test, though not representing a direct form of testing, was chosen because it is a good indicator of the students' acquisition of a variety of skills and sub-skills. Skills include reading and writing ability, and even oral ability if the text is a passage from a conversation and contains elements specific to oral communication. Provided that the text is carefully selected for its authenticity and its relevance to the course content and that the deleted words are well targeted, the cloze test can provide an accurate measurement of the students' progress and give useful feedback. Because it is an indirect type of testing, however, and does not reflect real life language use, students have to be familiarised with the task, which has to be included both in classroom activities and in the study packs.

From the tutors' point of view, writing good cloze tests and listening comprehensions can be difficult and time-consuming. In addition, part-time tutors working in various institutions can have very different views on the format and the content of these tests. In order to guide tutors through the process, and to ensure minimum parity across the languages, a Teacher's Guide was produced, which offers guidelines for the construction of all the tests, their administration and their marking. Language Co-ordinators also have an important part to play, mainly as advisers and quality controllers. Furthermore, training is essential and workshops on test writing and marking have been organised.

The marking of the cloze test and the listening comprehension is quite straightforward and objective, as all the items are determined in advance. Tutors are required to construct a detailed answer sheet to go with their paper. For the marking of the listening comprehension at beginners level (Stage 1), a scale was created because the nature of the task at that level meant that students were achieving unrealistically high marks. Indeed, as pointed out by Hughes (1989: 135), *'if the (listening) test is set at an appropriate level, then, as with reading, a near perfect set of responses may be required for a "pass".'* The scale is constructed on a 60:40 reference point, whereby students are expected to give a set of answers at least 60% correct in order to achieve the 40% pass mark.

Students get the feedback from the tests as they go through their marked papers with their tutor during the following class (Week 8) and discuss their performance.

Coursework 2

The second part of the assessment takes place at the end of the course during the last class (Week 13) and serves to evaluate whether students have acquired the linguistic and communicative skills required to complete a module successfully. It consists of two tests, one oral, one written, both testing directly the general abilities outlined in the course objectives. Constraints of time again had to be taken into account in the design of the tests: only 2H45 are available to test a class of sometimes up to eighteen students, thus restricting the number (and variety) of tasks that can be included.

For the oral test, a minimum of two tasks was needed, to reflect the importance given to speaking and listening skills in the course syllabus (see weighting in OLP assessment breakdown). Hence the choice of a role play followed by a interview-type conversation at beginners and lower inter-mediate levels (Stages 1/1, 1/2 and 2/1), and a topic-based discussion with a more personal conversation at higher intermediate and advanced levels (Stages 2/2, 3/1 and 3/2). Tasks of this nature (more transactional at lower stages, more interactional at higher stages) have been performed by students during their course and represent acts of communication they are expected to be able to perform in real life. Once again, for reasons of parity, both the role play and the controlled conversation (Stage 1) are standard-ised, with a choice of set topics and main points (functions) onto which tutors have to add elements specific to their course programmes. At the higher levels, tutors choose the topics for the discussion, taken from their course programme based on the general syllabus. Moreover, the length of the task is pre-determined for everybody.

The written test is also task-based, students having to write a letter or another form of written communication, like a postcard, a note, an e-mail, etc. As for the oral test, the format is outlined in the Teacher's Guide, so as to ensure that the same type of performance is required from all students at the same level — Russian and Greek having a separate format at beginners level, because of the extra time needed to learn the new script (this also applies to the cloze test).

To ensure consistent marking for the oral and written tests, marking grids were produced, to be used for all languages at all levels, and which can therefore be adapted to different criterial levels of performance. The criteria used for the oral tests are fluency, pronunciation, content, vocabulary and grammar, defined on a scale of 0 to 4, and those for the written tests are content, style, vocabulary and grammar, defined on a scale of 0 to 5.

Coursework 3

Lastly, to reflect the increased importance of the written element at Stages 2 and 3, there is an additional written assignment that students do in their own time, between Week 9 and Week 13. It consists in finding information from a document and reporting it in the target language, task corresponding directly to the objectives outlined in the course syllabus.

Evaluation of the system

Bachman and Palmer's 'plan for the evaluation of usefulness' (1996) offers a model which is both comprehensive and rigorous. The purpose here, however, is not to apply the plan in all its details, but to use its general principles for a qualitative analysis of the OLP system of assessment. The six qualities of usefulness outlined in the plan (reliability, construct validity, authenticity, interactiveness, impact and practicality) will form the basis for the analysis, with authenticity and interactiveness being merged in a single concept of 'communicative approach'.

We are dealing with 'high-stakes' achievement tests, and therefore a high level of reliability is needed, i.e. consistency in the measurement of the tests. Having in some cases multiple-class modules, with up to six different tutors correcting test papers, makes this more difficult to achieve, so standardisation of the design and the administration of the tests, as well as their scoring, is essential. To that effect, items included in the tests are as much as possible determined in advance, time allotment is specified for each level, and marking criteria are set up for each test. As far as the scoring of the written and oral tests is concerned, well-defined criteria are used by all tutors, but it is left to them to interpret them according to the level of their course module. Criterial levels of performance therefore need to be defined for each language at each level, based on set standards, to achieve greater consistency in grades awarded within and across languages and avoid excessive reliance on moderators and external examiners.

The principal aim of the tests being to measure the students' achievement, it is essential that the tests represent every aspect of the subject of assessment, in order to support the validity of scores interpretation. This is satisfied insofar as the number and variety of items in the test represent a good sample of the content of the course programmes, and as the test tasks are familiar to the students and require little use of non-linguistic abilities (such as organising arguments for an essay, for example). Moreover, scoring procedures are directly related to the course objectives, with criteria focused on the students' ability to communicate successfully.

Tests are in line with a communicative approach as tasks require authentic language use, within the limits imposed by the diversity in students' background. Likewise, tests are constructed using authentic materials, including for example well-defined context and purpose of communication. They are also interactive to some degree, listening comprehensions for instance including information transfer type of tasks, and oral and written tests leaving students some room to manoeuvre. However, they do not contain a great amount of unpredictability, as this would reduce reliability.

Positive impact is achieved by having tests known and understood by both students and tutors, which contain tasks consistent with the goals of the course and familiar to the students. In the case of multiple-class modules, when the same tests are shared by several tutors, positive impact depends to a large extent on effective team work. As far as marking is concerned, criteria are not systematically explained to students at present, as it is left to each tutor to mention them in greater or lesser details. A more uniform approach would certainly achieve better impact, and probably result in improved students' performance. Lastly, considerations of practicality unfortunately make it difficult to give students feedback from the final tests, although this can be obtained on an informal basis.

Given the size of the programme, it is essential that tests be easy and practical to construct, administer, score and interpret. As explained above, considerations of practicality have played an important part in the development of the system of assessment, as can be seen for example in the choice of the number and timing of test tasks. The main difficulty that exists for tutors of large classes is the time needed to administer the oral tests, as this is done on a one-to-one basis. This, however, was considered necessary for the authenticity and validity of the task (involving communication with a native speaker), as well as for its reliability (the alternative option, pairwork, leading to students influencing each other's performance).

Conclusion

As the evaluation of the OLP system of assessment has shown, there is no recipe for a perfect test, different situations requiring more or less emphasis on particular test characteristics. To achieve a system of assessment which is effective and has beneficial backwash on teaching and learning, it is therefore essential to adopt a critical approach for every stage of the development, the administration and the marking of the tests. This, of course, represents a significant task for tutors and administrators, for which time and resources must be allocated.

However, developing a sound system of assessment can benefit many aspects of a language programme. As far as course accreditation is concerned, assessment, by creating a need for clear objectives and standards, can help to achieve greater parity between languages. This is essential for departments of continuing education seeking to streamline language provision with the aim of making courses compatible to facilitate student and tutor mobility. From the tutors' point of view, the critical analysis of course programmes and methodologies, and the developmental work associated with testing can directly feed into their teaching, provided that both activities are well integrated. As for students, having well-defined course objectives and standards against which they can measure their progress can give them a better understanding and more control over their learning process.

Nevertheless, the introduction of a new system of assessment necessitates a cautious approach. In the case of continuing education, students' expectations rarely include being tested, and sometimes painful memories from schooldays can generate negative feelings towards assessment. For this reason, it is crucial to have students involved directly into the testing process, and to try to make it an activity that enhances their learning and enables them to achieve the best possible performance. As regards tutors, the allocation of time and resources must include appropriate training. For example, considering the size of most language programmes, the issue of reliability is very important, and ways have to be found to reach a maximum level of consistency between assessors. One way to achieve this is to organise sessions with tutors at each level to standardise the marking, following procedures similar to those adopted in the Language Programme of Leeds Metropolitan University (Zöllner, 1995). Finally, new avenues remain to be explored, such as self-assessment and peer-assessment, which have been found to benefit both learning and testing, by helping students to become more familiar with the nature of assessment tasks and criteria.

Bibliography

Bachman L F and A S Palmer, *Language testing in practice* (OUP, 1996)

Hughes A, *Testing for language teachers* (CUP, 1989)

Zöllner R, 'Standardisation across languages' presented at the Fifth National Institution-Wide Language Programmes Conference at The Nottingham Trent University, September 1995

Further reading

Bachman L F, 'What does language testing have to offer?' *TESOL Quarterly* (Vol 25, No. 4, 1991)

Cunningham D, 'CLOZE: a rationale for practical applications' *Language Learning Journal* (No. 12, 1995)

Race P, 'Four papers on assessment' presented at the AETT International Conference York. April 1992

Weir C, *Understanding and developing language tests* (Prentice Hall International, 1993)

Introducing credit and assessment: attitudes and responses among adult language learners

4

Ian McCall, University of Southampton

In 1994, when the Higher Education Funding Council for England (HEFCE) announced that in future students would have to be enrolled on accredited courses to qualify for funding, the former Department of Adult Continuing Education (DACE) of the University of Southampton had a large programme of liberal courses.[1] This included a wide range of popular and minority languages, from beginners level to approximately 'A' level, with a student body that on the whole did not seem particularly interested in gaining credit. The first part of this paper considers the processes we went through to accredit the languages programme. It outlines some of the internal and external constraints that influenced both the amount of credit that was attached to courses and the assessment scheme that was developed. The second part of the paper evaluates how students responded to credit and assessment. This is based on substantial data obtained from a questionnaire distributed to students on the newly accredited courses.

Background

In accrediting the adult education programme DACE had decided to award university rather than departmental credit. The decision had also been taken to fully adopt the principles of the Credit Accumulation Transfer Scheme (CATS), so that credit would have full currency within the university. In addition, it had been decided to accredit all courses at Level 1 or above under CATS and none at Level 0. These decisions were partially linked to concerns about future funding: it was unsure whether departmental credit would be sufficient to satisfy future HEFCE requirements and suspected that courses accredited below Level 1 might not continue to attract funding as they might be deemed to be pre-HE.

---

1 The Department of Adult Continuing Education has since become part of University of Southampton New College which was created on 1 September 1997.

The main implication of these decisions for the department was that it was necessary to seek formal approval through the academic standards mechanisms of the university for the accreditation of the programme. As in many other continuing education departments going through the same process, it was anticipated that there would be more than slight resistance from mainstream departments, where some colleagues were simply against the award of credit to adult education students. At Southampton, in order to pre-empt any unnecessary problems we chose to mirror mainstream departments as closely as possible, especially in terms of the amount of credit given in relation to contact hours and the amount of assessment required to receive credit. Adult education needed to be able to argue the case convincingly that the effort required from students on its courses was equivalent to that demanded of mainstream students for a similar amount of credit and that we would not be simply giving credit away and compromising university standards. In arts subjects, this meant adopting the formula that a unit of fifteen CATS points required 24 contact hours and a further 96 private study hours and that assessment should be through either approximately 3,000 words of assessed written work, a three-hour exam, or an equivalent hybrid of methods.

Faced with the above formula, several options were open to us. One solution would have been to attach fewer credit points to course units and scale down the amount of assessment accordingly. We could, for example, have given a course unit five credit points instead of fifteen and reduced the quantity of assessment by two thirds. This solution seemed risky, however, as there was uncertainty at the time concerning how continuing education might be funded in the future. The prevailing view seemed to be that funding would be credit rather than contact-hour based, which would mean that by attaching only five credit points to course units of 24 contact hours we would receive only a third of the funding under such an arrangement. In order to remain financially viable we would then have had to make a further case to the university to have the credit rating on courses increased and had to justify why essentially the same courses were now worthy of more credit points.

Another quick fix solution would have been to give students an optional examination after each unit, thereby keeping the teaching and assessment processes separate, as is frequently the case in mainstream provision. But we suspected that most of our students were not particularly interested in the credit and that the likely outcome would have been a very low uptake. In the short term this would not have mattered had there not been fears that future funding might be linked to participation rates. We concluded that we should do our best to maximise uptake, or at least get students used to the idea of assessment, so we could take a firmer line if HEFCE subsequently introduced outcome funding.

Having decided to follow patterns from other parts of the university and adopted the 15 credit point/24 contact hour ratio we set about attempting to translate the assessment requirements into equivalents that were more appropriate and palpable for adults studying languages, many at beginners level. We optimistically adopted the approach that if we had to include assessment we should at least try to make its effects as positive as possible for both students and staff. Therefore, in undertaking our translation exercise we decided that if assessment was to have beneficial backwash on learning and teaching, any scheme we devised should be guided by the following basic principles. [2] It should:

- be an essential part of the learning experience itself;
- be fully integrated into the course, rather than merely 'bolted on' as an administrative necessity;
- be related directly to the course objectives;
- take place at regular intervals allowing students to develop their skills of self-assessment and monitor their progress;
- be designed in such a way as to motivate students to achieve the course objectives;
- give students a clear indication as to whether they were ready to move on;
- result in better standards of achievement.

Two other factors also influenced our scheme. The first was we were going to be working fully within the CATS system and therefore required by the university to give our students precise marks at the end of the course to indicate their performance. The second was that as we were offering HE credit at Level 1 in a modular framework the university required that all courses be subject to an examination board with concrete evidence of student work provided. This meant, in short, that adopting one of the criterion-referenced type assessment schemes that are popular now for many adult language courses was not a possibility as such schemes merely pass or fail students. Any type of assessment scheme whereby tutors merely tick boxes on checklists would also be out of the question as these did not provide sufficient concrete evidence of students' achievements. [3]

As our part-time tutors were to be at the forefront of implementing assessment and we desperately needed their support and co-operation, we decided to involve them as far as possible in the creation of the assessment schemes. [4] As expected many tutors were initially apprehensive about the

---

2   An explanation of the term *backwash* and other terminology relating to assessment can be found in Hughes A, *Testing for language teachers*, (CUP, 1989).

3   Examples of this type of scheme can be found in Ainslie S and A Lamping, *Assessing adult learners*, (CILT, 1995); see p.13.

4   An account of the discussions we had are given in my article in *Netword*, No. 15, Spring, 1994, p.5.

accreditation and assessment of courses. They feared that students would be traumatised by the thought of being 'tested', find the classes less enjoyable and vote with their feet. But faced with the fact they had no real choice, tutors seemed on the whole to prefer to be provided with prescriptive guidelines on how and what to assess rather than being merely left to their own devices. Given the sheer size of the languages programme, and the fact that it was being run by only 1.5 staff, it also seemed wise from an administrative point of view to create generic systems for all languages rather than allow tutors complete freedom, which would have been difficult to manage and would have resulted in unjustifiable inconsistencies across languages.

The assessment scheme

The liberal programme was structured into six language levels, ranging from beginners at Level 1 to approximately 'A' level standard at Level 6. Each level comprised 24 two-hour meetings. Weeks 1–12 were Unit A, Weeks 13–24 Unit B of the course. Each unit was worth fifteen CATS points and was to be assessed separately. After consultation with part-time tutors it was decided to adopt schemes for all levels that were based heavily on short but frequent objective tests and assessed homework. The rationale behind this approach was that if assessment occurred frequently in class time students would be more encouraged to participate in the scheme. It was also thought that frequent, regular assessment tasks would motivate students to undertake the homestudy that we all agreed was necessary to make real progress. If the tasks were administered in class they could also be used (in the subsequent session) for revision and to give students feedback on how they were doing. In the first year of the scheme some marks were also allocated to attendance at Levels 1–4 to give less experienced language learners confidence that they would probably pass if they attended regularly and undertook some assessment tasks. (The marks attributed to attendance have since been reduced and will be phased out.)

The following scheme outlines how Levels 3 and 4 were assessed. It is followed by some comments on the variations for Levels 1, 2, 5 and 6.

- *Attendance* (20%): Students received 1% per tuition hour attended up to 20% maximum.

- *Listening skills* (20%): assessed by two short listening comprehension tests per unit of about twenty minutes each. (Tests took place in Meetings 6 and 12 for Unit A and Meetings 18 and 23 for Unit B.)

- *Writing and reading skills*: assessed by two short listening comprehension tests per unit of about 30 minutes each. (Tests took place in Meetings 6 and 12 for Unit A and Meetings 18 and 23 for Unit B.)

- *Assessed written homework* (20%): Assessed by four short pieces per unit.

- *Oral skills* (20%): Assessed by a short talk (10%) and tutor appraisal (10%).

At Levels 1 and 2 fewer pieces of assessed homework were required and in addition to the longer writing and reading tests there were two short vocabulary tests to encourage students to learn vocabulary regularly. Oral skills were assessed less formally by tutor appraisal according to stated criteria. At Levels 5 and 6 students were expected to undertake three substantial pieces of assessed homework and to do a longer class talk followed by questions from the class.

As most of our tutors had never had any experience of designing assessment tasks we created a small working group to draw up specimens so tutors had models to work to. This was to ensure that at each level assessment tasks were relevant to the course objectives, fun to do, varied, visually attractive and that there was consistency across languages. We suggested, for example, that at lower levels pictures and diagrams might be included to make the tasks less intimidating. We also allowed students, where necessary, to use their own paper so that they did not feel that they were sitting examinations. If students seemed to be having difficulty completing the tasks in the allocated time tutors were also allowed to increase it slightly on the spur of the moment to avoid an examination room atmosphere.

Presenting assessment to students

Once the assessment scheme had been designed the next task was to decide a strategy for selling it to students, many of whom would have already attended liberal courses with us. It seemed best to allow tutors to explain the assessment scheme once in the classroom rather than outlining it at length in the syllabus students receive before starting their course. In the latter we simply stated: 'Every student who wishes to be awarded the credit for his or her language studies will be asked to undertake the necessary assessment. Assessment is directly related to class work and has been designed to be student-friendly'. Indeed, we were afraid that if we included too much about assessment in the syllabus students would simply not enrol. In order to prepare tutors for presenting assessment to students we undertook a staff development session in which we rehearsed the arguments in favour of assessing and considered strategies for dealing with students who might be resistant and claim that it was a waste of time. As in all good language teaching there was some role play.

The university requires that before courses start or at the beginning of courses students receive explicit documentation outlining the methods of assessment and when assessment will take place. We put these details in a brochure that tutors would distribute to students. But more important, as an aid to tutors, we decided to include in this brochure remarks stressing the value of assessment. We emphasised how the scheme was designed to motivate students to study at home, to provide feedback on progress and allow students to identify areas and topics that required further consolidation. We also stated that by undertaking the tasks students would have a better idea at the end of the level whether they were ready for the next one. We also stressed how receiving a transcript with the credit points could give students a sense of personal satisfaction at the end of a stimulating period of study, or provide evidence of achievement for an employer. In short, the brochure was treated as a sales document and rather than using dreary white paper, colourful, visually attractive covers were used. In addition, in these brochures it was made clear that students were free to opt out of some or all of the assessment tasks or could do them informally. This meant that students could attempt tasks but not hand them in for marking, or could ask a tutor to correct them without awarding a mark if they did not want the credit. (It was implied, however, that it was educationally more desirable for students to follow the assessment scheme more rigidly.)

Implementing assessment: initial reactions

Some tutors had been preparing their students for the introduction of the scheme in the previous year and the fact that recruitment had not been affected too drastically led to initial optimism. But shortly after courses had started things took a dramatic turn for the worse, especially around Week 6 when the first assessment tasks were due to take place. Some tutors were stressed at having had to produce tests, thinking that if they made them too difficult their students might get bad marks and desert their courses. Other tutors had spent sleepless nights agonising over what mark to award pieces of assessed work. Some had had to deal with irate students who did not want credit and thought that assessment was a waste of teaching time and had resulted in higher course fees. Other students were undertaking the tasks out of loyalty to the tutor but making it clear that they did not enjoy the course as much as in the past. Some tutors were just annoyed with the extra work they felt they were doing without being sufficiently paid. It was in this climate that we decided to undertake a survey of our students.

The questionnaire

Rationale behind the questionnaire and its administration

Our aims in distributing the questionnaire were threefold. Firstly, we wanted to gain valuable information on the composition of our student body.

Secondly, we wanted to see how far the negative feedback we were receiving from some tutors and students was justified. Thirdly, and perhaps most important, we wanted to give students the opportunity to express any grievances and to make them realise that we were willing to make changes if necessary. We told tutors that once the questionnaire had been completed they might take the opportunity to tell students that we were aware that there were some teething problems and would be making changes for the next academic year. The questionnaire would help us with this. The questionnaire was distributed in February 1996, in Meeting 13, the first class after students had been through the entire assessment process for Unit A.

Questionnaire content and results

In addition to providing us with information on student attitudes to assessment and credit, we wanted to use the questionnaire to see how far age, sex, educational background, or even the ability to speak another foreign language in addition to the one studied influenced students' attitude to assessment. Therefore, before considering the responses to the questions relating specifically to assessment and credit it is pertinent to give some information concerning the nature of our student body.

The response rate to the questionnaire was high. Of potentially 400 students enrolled on the courses surveyed we received 268 responses, spread over 28 courses. This represents a response rate of 67% and an average response of 9.57 per course of a potential average of 14.28. As the questionnaires were completed in one particular session some students may have been absent for justifiable reasons. It can be assumed that in Week 13 over 70% of students were still attending the courses. It cannot be ignored, however, that some students may have dropped out because they were put off by the idea of being assessed. 49% of students were studying at Levels 1 or 2, 33% at Levels 3 or 4 and 18% at Levels 5 or 6.

In terms of the profile of our student body the percentage of men on our courses seemed to dispel the myth that languages are more popular with women (45% men, 55% women). We had always suspected that our student body was educated but not to the extent revealed by the data: 90% of respondents had at least 'A' levels or equivalent and 70% of all respondents were graduates. In terms of the age profile of students 11.6% were under 25, 38.1% between 25 and 45, 44% between 46 and 65 and 6.3% over 65. [5]

---

5   Our student body in languages seemed quite similar to that outlined in a 1996 NIACE survey. See Tuckett A and N Sargant, 'Creating Two Nations?': Headline Findings on Lifelong Learning from NIACE/GALLUP Survey 1996', (NIACE, 1996), p.7.

Our marketing office had stressed the exciting, positive aspects of credit and the CATS scheme in a large amount of publicity materials. The questionnaire asked directly: *Did you enrol on the course specifically because credit was being offered?* Only 4.5% of students ticked the *yes* box in response to this question with an overwhelming 95.5% ticking *no*. It was a little disappointing at a time when we had been forced to accredit language courses that so few students seemed to actually want the credit.

As stated above, we had aimed to maximise the number of students participating in the assessment scheme. Our strategy had been successful. In response to the question *Did you participate in any aspect of the assessment scheme?*, 87% of respondents ticked *yes* and only 13% ticked *no*. A smaller number of students (67%) ticked *yes* in response to the question: *Are you claiming the credit for the language unit you have just completed?* In fact there was a difference of 50 students who did some form of assessment but opted out. It is difficult to interpret this data. Some students may have wanted to do one aspect of the assessment (like the class talk, or assessed homework) but not enough for them to want to be given the credit, possibly through fear of gaining a low mark. Others may have completed the assessments but then declined the credit. (We know that some students did all the tasks but then refused the credit as a form of protest to show that they considered the credit of little value!)

In terms of attitudes towards assessment and our scheme in particular students were asked to tick boxes in the following table which has been extracted from the questionnaire:

	strongly agree	agree	uncertain	disagree	strongly disagree
I was concerned about the prospect of assessment at the beginning of the course.					
The assessment scheme has improved my learning of the language.					
The assessment scheme has reduced my enjoyment of the course.					
The assessment scheme has increased my motivation to learn the language.					
Looking back, I am pleased that I participated in the assessment scheme.					

Tutors were concerned that students would be scared by the prospect of assessment and that it would put them off. The response to the statement *I was concerned about the prospect of assessment at the beginning of the course* did not confirm this, as these statistics show:

Value Label	Frequency	Valid %	Cum. %
strongly agree	17	6.5	6.5
agree	57	21.7	28.1
uncertain	56	21.3	49.4
disagree	79	30	79.5
strongly disagree	54	20.5	100

There are several explanations for these figures. Either tutors had done an impressive job reassuring students, or the fact that 90% of respondents had been educated to at least 'A' level or equivalent meant that our system seemed much less stressful to students who had probably undertaken long formal examinations.

When cross-tabulated against other information our data also revealed that there were no significant differences between the age groups in response to this question. But there was a significant difference between those who did and those who did not speak another foreign language in addition to the one being studied. Those who spoke another language were much less likely to express concern at the prospect of assessment. We also noted that students studying minority languages were significantly less concerned about the prospect of assessment than those learning popular languages. Perhaps the latter had been subjected to negative experiences of assessment at school like the dreaded French test!

We had hoped that students would perceive a notable difference in their progress as a result of incorporating assessment. The response to *The assessment scheme has improved my learning of the language* was not as positive as we would have wished:

Value Label	Frequency	Valid %	Cum. %
strongly agree	19	7.2	7.2
agree	94	35.7	43
uncertain	65	24.7	67.7
disagree	57	21.7	89.4
strongly disagree	28	10.6	100

The younger age groups (<46 years) and full-time students were significantly more likely to say that the assessment scheme had improved their learning of the language, as were those who had enrolled on the course specifically because credit was being offered. Students who had never attended a language course since leaving school were also more likely to agree that the assessment scheme had improved their learning. The implication is that those who had attended an unassessed language course in the past perceived little real improvement to their learning as result of assessment.

Tutors had always been concerned that students would enjoy their courses less when assessment was introduced and many claimed that that this was the message they were receiving from their students. We were quite relieved to find, however, that 55.5% of students disagreed with *The assessment scheme has reduced my enjoyment of the course* as opposed to 27.8% agreeing:

Value Label	Frequency	Valid %	Cum. %
strongly agree	26	9.9	9.9
agree	47	17.9	27.8
uncertain	44	16.7	44.5
disagree	97	36.9	81.4
strongly disagree	49	18.6	100

The younger age groups (<46 years) were significantly less likely to say that the assessment scheme had reduced their enjoyment of the course. Those having attended other language courses since leaving school were significantly more likely to say that the assessment scheme had reduced their enjoyment. What is interesting, however, is that there was barely any difference in this response between those who had attended a course with us and those who had followed courses elsewhere.

Our tutors and our brochure had emphasised how the assessment scheme was designed to motivate students. The response to *The assessment scheme has increased my motivation to learn the language* was therefore disappointing, with more students disagreeing rather than agreeing:

Value Label	Frequency	Valid %	Cum. %
strongly agree	19	7.2	7.7
agree	80	30.4	37.6
uncertain	41	15.6	53.2
disagree	84	31.9	85.2
strongly disagree	39	14.8	100

Again, younger students (<46 years) were significantly more likely to say that the assessment scheme had increased their motivation.

The final remark *Looking back I am pleased that I participated in the assessment scheme* did give us more cause for optimism:

Value Label	Frequency	Valid %	Cum. %
strongly agree	28	11.1	11.1
agree	112	44.3	55.3
uncertain	50	19.8	75.1
disagree	26	14.6	89.7
strongly disagree	39	10.3	100

Consistent with the trend noted above younger people (<46 years) were significantly more pleased that they participated in the assessment scheme. Employed people were also significantly more pleased than other groups that they had participated.

The questionnaire also elicited information concerning students' views regarding the amount of assessment. The following is extracted from the questionnaire:

The amount of assessment was . . . .*(please tick the appropriate boxes)*

	too high	too low	about right
. . . for the class test	☐	☐	☐
. . . for home assignments	☐	☐	☐
. . . overall	☐	☐	☐

Tutors had consistently argued that students were unhappy with the amount of assessment. This does not seem to be confirmed by the data:

The amount of assessment for the class tests was:

Value Label	Frequency	Valid %	Cum. %
too high	54	22.1	22.1
too low	2	0.8	23.0
about right	188	77	77

The amount of assessment for home assignments was:

Value Label	Frequency	Valid %	Cum. %
too high	35	14.5	4.5
too low	12	5.0	19.5
about right	194	80.5	100.0

The amount of assessment overall was:

Value Label	Frequency	Valid %	Cum. %
too high	41	17.4	17.4
too low	2	0.8	18.2
about right	193	81.8	100

We can safely assume that most of the 13% who did not participate in the scheme would have ticked too high. If we disregard this figure the vast majority of the students did not seem to object to the actual amount of assessment.

Conclusion

The above data does not suggest that the majority of students were against assessment, as some part-time tutors had led us to believe. What is evidently clear, however, is that there was a significant number of students who were unhappy with the inclusion of assessment and many who did not perceive that it had any positive effects on their learning experience. The fact that tutors may have had to devote time and energy to disgruntled students, who are often more vocal than satisfied ones, may have poisoned the atmosphere in the classroom and undermined tutor confidence and job satisfaction. Indeed, a few of the very negative comments in the free answer section of the questionnaire revealed that some tutors may have had to deal with some very dissatisfied customers.

On the positive side, many tutors noted a marked improvement in the progress their students made and their own teaching. They felt that having to devise assessment tasks in advance meant that they had to have a clearer idea of where they were going rather than allowing the course to set its own pace. However, tutors were concerned that the word assessment was omnipresent and that it pervaded their courses.

In the light of the fact that outcome funding seemed less likely, for the following year we reduced the frequency of assessment tasks. Instead of having two Meetings per unit in which tasks took place, we had one meeting which was more or less devoted to a larger number of tasks. The atmosphere in the classes is now less divided and students who do not want credit simply tend to miss the meeting devoted to assessment, rather than feeling they are missing a substantial part of the course which was the case in the previous year.

Acknowledgements

I would like to thank my colleagues Ian Bryant and Jackie Ross for giving invaluable help with both the design of the questionnaire and the interpretation of data.

Translation to assess language competence: present and future

5

Sara Laviosa, University of Birmingham

In this paper, I will first of all analyse three main definitions of translation put forward in Translation Studies from the mid 1960s to the early 1990s, each of which reflects a particular underlying theoretical model of the product and the process of translation. I will then report on how translation is currently used as a means of assessing linguistic competence in my institution: the Modern Languages Unit of the University of Birmingham, and examine the relationship between these practices and the three models of translation put forward in the first part of the paper. Finally, I will propose to draw on the cultural and functionalist models of translation to devise new classroom activities aimed at developing and assessing the cultural and pragmatic competence of adult foreign language learners.

Three definitions and three models of translation

One of the most well known definitions of translation which captures the linguistic aspects of translating is the one put forward by Catford (1965). He defines translation as *'the replacement of textual material in one language (SL) by equivalent textual material in another language (TL)'* (Catford, 1965: 20). Translation is therefore conceived as an operation performed on languages, a unidirectional and direct process of substituting a text in one language for a text in another. This view emphasises the role played by the source and the target language systems, and centres around the importance of maintaining what Nida (1964: 159) calls *'formal equivalence'* between the source and the target text, which he intends as the reproduction of both the content and the form of the source language text, so that the sentence boundaries, punctuation marks and paragraph breaks of the original text are retained in the translation. An example of this type of translation is the series of parallel texts published by Penguin. Each book in the series contains original short stories or extracts from novels written in a foreign language together with translations into English which closely reproduce both the content and the formal aspects of the source texts. These books are addressed to learners of a foreign language and the function of the translations is to help the reader understand the individual words and structures of the original text.

Towards the end of the 1960s, particularly under the influence of Bible translators, theorists began to feel dissatisfied with Catford's linguistic model, which could account only for a narrow range of translation activities. In 1969, Reverend Eugene Nida put forward a new and more complex model of the translation process which is reflected in the following definition: *'Translating consists in reproducing in the receptor language the closest natural equivalent of the source-language message, first in terms of meaning and secondly in terms of style'* (Nida and Taber, 1969/1982: 12).

While Catford uses the notion of textual material, Nida uses the concept of message. While Catford emphasises formal equivalence, that is the correspondence of both form and content, Nida introduces the contrasting idea of *'dynamic equivalence'*, which is the correspondence of message, so that *'the response of the receptor is essentially like that of the original receptors'* (Nida and Taber, 1969/1982: 200, emphasis removed). It follows that in a dynamically equivalent translation, the translator will substitute culturally obscure source language words and concepts with words and notions that are meaningful and relevant to the target language culture. An example of this type of equivalence is offered by the translation of the biblical phrase *'Lamb of God'* into an Eskimo language with the phrase *'Seal of God'* (Snell-Hornby 1988/1995: 19).

The model of translating which informs Nida's proposed definition of translation and notion of dynamic equivalence includes three main phases: Analysis, Transfer, and Restructuring (Nida and Taber, 1969/1982: 104). In the first stage, the translator *'analyses the message of the source language into its simplest and structurally clearest form'* (Nida, 1969: 484). He or she then mentally transfers the message at this level from language A to language B, modifying it, as necessary, according to the requirements of the target language structures (Nida and Taber, 1969/1982: 39). Finally, in the restructuring phase, the translator transforms the results of the transfer process into a *'stylistic form appropriate to the receptor language and to the intended receptors'* (Nida and Taber, 1969/1982: 206).

One of the most notable innovations of Nida's cultural approach to translation is the recognition of the role of the translator as an intercultural mediator, who is therefore required to have *'not only a bilingual ability but also a bi-cultural vision'* (Hatim and Mason, 1990: 223). However, Nida's model still centres around the importance of maintaining some form of equivalence between the source and the target text, namely the preservation of the original impact in the source language culture. This may indeed be true for a large number of translations, but not all of them. As Nord observes, *'professional translating includes many cases where equivalence is not called for at all'* Nord (1997: 8). An example is provided by the well known children's book *The Arabian Nights*, whose original text in Arabic is strictly intended for an adult audience, and rich in sexual allusions. Translation theorists, particularly those involved in translator training, felt that a new approach was called for, one which could account also for the exceptions from the equivalence requirement. The functionalist approach, developed by Katharina Reiß and Hans Vermeer mainly in the late 1970s and early 1980s, arises as a response to this need. Functionalists view translation as a purposeful activity governed by the intended function of the target text or any of its parts. It is from a functionalist perspective that Nord (1991: 28), one of the leading theorists in the field today, puts forward the following definition of translation, the third and last being reviewed here. According to Nord, *'translation is the production of a functional target text maintaining a relationship with a given source text that is specified according to the intended or demanded function of the target text (translation skopos)'* (Nord, 1991: 28), where the skopos is the goal or purpose of the translation determined by the translation brief, which is negotiated between the client and the translator.

The two main novelties of the functionalist approach are a) the rejection of equivalence as an *a priori*, therefore the recognition of the possibility that the translated text may have a different communicative purpose from the original text and b) the incorporation of two additional elements in the model of translation: the role of the initiator of the translation process and the skopos of the translation. The theoretical model underlying the new view of translation identifies the relations existing between the most important features that characterise translation, as well as its place within the general network of concepts concerning other types of intentional behaviours. As we can see from the diagrammatic representation of this model opposite (Nord, 1997: 18), translation is an intentional, bi-directional, interpersonal, communicative, mediated, and intercultural action based on a source text.

It can be argued that, as we progress from Catford's linguistic approach to Nida's cultural model, and finally to Nord's functionalist perspective the different models put forward by translation theorists are able to account for a wider and wider range of authentic translational activities. As a consequence, the gulf between theory and practice within the discipline has been progressively narrowed.

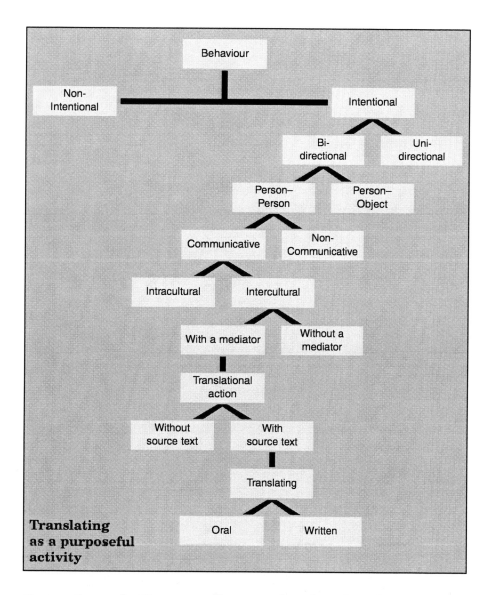

Behaviour

Non-Intentional

Intentional

Bi-directional

Uni-directional

Person–Person

Person–Object

Communicative

Non-Communicative

Intracultural

Intercultural

With a mediator

Without a mediator

Translational action

Without source text

With source text

Translating

Translating as a purposeful activity

Oral

Written

From translation studies to the foreign language classroom and back (the present)

I will now leave aside the models elaborated within the discipline of Translation Studies and move onto a different and more specific area of study: the foreign language classroom for adult learners in one particular institution, namely the Modern Languages Unit (MLU) of the University of Birmingham. Here my aim is to discover whether translation is used as a means of assessing linguistic competence, and if so, to what extent, and why. My research questions follow on from two previous studies (Laviosa-

Braithwaite, 1996; 1997) in which I have examined the use of translation in a number of British and American universities in the particular context of Italian as a foreign language (IFL).

Before I report on the methodology and the results of my study, I would like to point out that the general policy adopted at the MLU on the use of translation in language testing requires that the translational task be carried out into English, providing this is the students' mother tongue. Compared with what generally occurs in the language departments of the old and new universities throughout the Country this position is quite innovative and indeed in line with the views and practices prevailing in professional translating (Laviosa-Braithwaite, 1996; 1997).

Methodology

My data have been elicited via a questionnaire (see Appendix 2, p117) which was kindly completed by my four colleagues who are the language co-ordinators for French, German, Spanish, and Russian.

Results

Only one of my colleagues uses translation for assessing language competence. She uses translation-based tasks from Level 1 up to and including Level 6 of our general language courses. The materials consist of individual sentences, paragraphs, phrases, and expressions. The sources are mixed: some texts are created by herself, while others are realia or have been selected from textbooks. The genres of the authentic texts are: literature, advertising, magazines, newspapers, instructions, descriptions of places, and the transcripts of dialogues on audio- and videotapes. The specific benefit that she attributes to translation as a means of testing language competence lies on the fact that translation *'gives an **exact meaning** of a given phrase, sentence, etc, and also helps students **feel language**'* (my emphasis).

Another colleague declared that he did at one time use translational tasks, but he no longer does so because of the multinational composition of his language classes, which makes translation into English impossible. When further questioned about what he would do if his class were entirely composed of native English speakers he replied, like the first colleague, that he would use translation at all levels of linguistic competence. The materials would consist mainly of sentences and unabridged texts, either created by himself or extracted from authentic publications. Among these, he would tend to prefer newspapers. The benefits he attributes to translation-based tasks are varied. Translation is believed to help explain **specific grammar points**. It also enables learners to **understand the text** better and it raises awareness of the **structural** and **semantic differences** between the source and the target language. Finally, it helps students appreciate that translating, contrary to common assumptions, is a **creative** rather than a mechanical or passive activity.

The opinions expressed by the two colleagues seem to emphasise the linguistic gains that learners derive from translating. Their main considerations centre around the importance of the formal aspects of the two languages in contact, namely the grammatical structures and the semantic systems. We can reasonably infer that the implicit model of translation which informs their views presents close parallels with the linguistic approach proposed by Catford (1965), which stresses the notion of formal equivalence between a source language text and its translation.

The other two colleagues do not make use of translation for language testing at all. One of them believes that *'translation is a very specific skill that most students [enroling on general language courses] are not interested in acquiring'*. The other tutor is of the opinion that *'language competence is best assessed in the foreign language, rather than by translating into or from it'*. Both these views seem to be informed by the belief that the translation process and the assessment of language competence belong to two separate subject fields in the general area of Applied Linguistics, therefore they should also be kept apart in practice. This opinion is shared by many theorists and practitioners working in Translation Studies and language teaching methodology respectively.

Interestingly, the spectrum of ideas revealed by this small scale study matches fairly closely the range of opinions expressed by a sample of 22 British and 16 American university lecturers of Italian as a foreign language for anglophones, who were the subjects of a previous survey (Laviosa-Braithwaite, 1997).

Generally speaking, and ignoring for the moment the subtle differences found between Britain and USA, there seem to be two distinct opinions on this subject. On the one hand, the supporters of translation in the foreign language classroom maintain that the benefit students derive from translating is their greater understanding of the formal aspects of the foreign language and a better appreciation of the grammatical and lexical differences between the source and the target language. On the other hand, those who do not use translation, either in the course of their teaching or for assessment purposes, believe that this act of language mediation ought to be kept separate from language teaching because they consider it to be alien to the learning process, therefore ineffective, if not even damaging.

Translation as a means of assessing cultural competence (the future)

I would now like to propose a new approach to translation, one which draws on the insights of the cultural and functionalist perspectives (see Nida's and Nord's models mentioned earlier) and originally applies them in the teaching of adult foreign language learners with the aim of developing and assessing not only their linguistic ability, but most importantly, their cultural and pragmatic competence in the foreign language.

What follows is an outline of the type of translational activities that I would like to develop to achieve these pedagogic objectives.

The students and the materials

The type of scenario I am envisaging consists of an anglophone class composed of adult learners studying Italian as a foreign language either at Level 5 or 6. For those who are unfamiliar with our system of accreditation and student allocation, I will briefly explain that students who enrol at Level 5 wish to further their Italian language skills in more advanced areas of competence and will have had at least 200 hours' previous tuition. Level 6 is suitable for those with a rusty 'A' level wishing to develop and extend advanced Italian language skills to a more sophisticated level. In both classes, learners extend their knowledge of Italian culture and should understand complex spoken language in various contexts as well as be able to extract and apply information, ideas and opinions, and communicate effectively in writing.

The material I would use in my activities consists of two authentic texts: one is an original Italian text, the other is its translation into English. Given the students' advanced level of linguistic competence, the activities would be explained and carried out entirely in Italian, except, of course for the translation itself, which would be in their mother tongue or language of habitual use.

The task

Phase 1

During the first phase I would distribute the Italian text, introducing it with a brief description of the genre it represents, where it was taken from, and its function in the source culture. I would then give the students more specific details about the assignment itself, namely the type of translation they are required to carry out (for example whether it is a complete or partial translation, or a summary); the mode of the translation (written or oral); the time allocated for the completion of the task; the presumed audience of the translation, and the function of the target text in the target culture. Dictionaries, thesauri, brochures, promotional publications, and any other kind of reference material which would be useful for the particular task in hand would be available for consultation. After the brief, the students would be asked to work in small groups and produce an annotated translated text, where they would describe the main difficulties they have encountered and the reasons for their proposed solution. At this stage my role would be to answer any queries that may arise about the lexico-grammatical aspects of the text, the register, the idioms, and the target culture.

Phase 2

The second phase involves comparing the translations produced by the different groups and to reach a consensus on the ones that seem to be the most suitable according to the principle of dynamic equivalence, if appropriate, or according to the effectiveness of the target text, assessed in terms of the skopos, which will have been determined by the assignment brief.

Phase 3

During the third and final phase, I would distribute the authentic translation of the original text so that we could all compare it both with the source text and the best translations produced by the students. The aim of this exercise would be to analyse the extent to which the authentic and the students' target texts differ from the original (for example there may be shifts in meaning caused by the substitution of source language hyponyms with target language hyperonyms; omissions; explicitations, etc) and discuss the possible reasons for such divergencies from a linguistic, cultural, and pragmatic point of view. I must stress that the real-life translation would not be introduced as a model to be imitated, but as an example of the type of work which is produced by professional translators, from which one can learn about the cultural and pragmatic differences existing between the two languages in contact.

With minor changes these basic procedures can also be used for self-, continuous, and classroom assessment. In the latter case, the evaluation of the individual translations would be carried out by two tutors. The class tutor would judge the translation according to the criteria described in Phase 2 and would allocate 70% of the final grade. The second tutor would allocate 30% of the grade. He or she would be either a native speaker of English or English would be his or her language of habitual use. He or she would only have access to the translations and the briefs, not to the original text. This is because his or her task would be to evaluate the target language text on the basis of its effectiveness as a piece of original writing in the target language culture.

Examples of texts that could be used for either classroom activities or tests are the multilingual translations of the descriptions and instructions that accompany imported products, such as food, cosmetics, stationery items, computer equipment, and so on. Other sources, over and above the commercial ones, are the bilingual in-flight magazines which publish parallel texts on a variety of subjects; tourist booklets, brochures and pamphlets; business correspondence (providing the names of the companies involved are removed for reasons of confidentiality), EU reports; opera, and pop songs. Translated literature and non-fiction also offer a vast range of texts at all levels of difficulty, as well as dubbed or subtitled films, and documentary scripts.

In fact we only need to pay close attention to the published and oral material that we encounter in our every-day life to realise that a considerable proportion of these consists of translated texts which could be fruitfully used in the foreign language classroom.

I believe that the activities outlined in this paper can enrich not only the linguistic competence of adult language learners, but, most importantly, their awareness of the cultural and pragmatic conventions prevailing in the foreign language country, while at the same time bring to light some very important aspects of the complex and fascinating process of real-life translating.

Bibliography

Catford J C, *A linguistic theory of translation: an essay in applied linguistics* (OUP, 1965)

Hatim B and I Mason, *Discourse and the translator* (Longman, 1990)

Laviosa-Braithwaite S, 'Translation in the Italian classroom: an exercise in contrastive grammar or an act of language mediation?' in The Proceedings of the AATI Annual Conference 11–13 December 1995, *Il Veltro*, Special Edition, 1996

Laviosa-Braithwaite S, 'Didattizzare la traduzione per acculturare e comunicare' in *Italica* 74 (4) 1997

Nida E A, 'Science of Translation' in *Language 45 (3)* 1969

Nida E A and C R Taber, *The theory and practice of translation* (Leiden: E J Brill, 1969/1982)

Nord C, *Text analysis in translation. Theory, methodology, and didactic application of a model for translation-oriented text analysis* (Amsterdam and Atlanta: Rodopi, 1991)

Nord C, *Translating as a purposeful activity: functionalist approaches explained* (St Jerome Publishing 1997)

Snell-Hornby M, *Translation studies: an integrated approach* (Amsterdam and Philadelphia: John Benjamins Publishing Company, 1988/1995)

Communicative assessment for adult learners: carrying coals to Newcastle?

6 Linda Hartley and Marion Spöring, University of Dundee

The mandatory introduction of accredited programmes in continuing education to an often sceptical and reluctant student body, as well as to a less sceptical albeit still reluctant group of language tutors, has challenged programme co-ordinators in CE Departments to introduce appropriate assessment mechanisms and tasks. Many departments, no doubt, had previously offered externally-validated examinations for the keen adult language learner. Informal assessment had also taken place, we imagine, in many language classes.

We would be considered to be strangely out of touch were we to question the methodology of CE practitioners: the majority would no doubt swear on the bible of communicative orthodoxy. It is well documented, however, that when teaching practice and policy changes, as they have done, this does not necessarily mean that assessment practice changes at the same time or at the same rate. Our doubts as to the type of assessments set by tutors then may be well founded.

> *'Methods of assessment tend to evolve more slowly than syllabuses (sic) and working practices.'* (Sewell, in Hawkins, 1996: 64)

Traditionally, most CE classes have been taught by part-time tutors. Some might be full-time teachers elsewhere, but a high percentage of them are without access to staff development in a full-time work environment. [1]

---

1 In Dundee, the Institute for Education and Lifelong Learning and the Centre for Applied Language Studies work with the same part-timers in appropriate languages and offer them a joint staff development programme. Since October 1997 they also have the option to study for a postgraduate Certificate in Teaching Modern Languages to Adults, offered by IELL.
   Part-timers, employed by both departments in the same languages (IELL currently offers 5, CALS 4 languages on an accredited basis), constitute more than half of the tutors employed in those accredited languages which both departments have in common. The staff turnover is, therefore, relatively low, despite the high number of part-timers employed, continuously at approximately 85% in the past 4 years.

This fact provides the first challenge of providing appropriate staff training aimed at part timers. A second challenge relates to the fact that traditional mainstream university language teaching and assessment have been dominated by an accuracy-centred approach (i.e. using grammar-translation methods). This approach is still in use in some mainstream Modern Languages departments and is one to which many tutors will have been exposed. This factor has been mentioned by Klapper (1997) and is also discussed in Coleman (1997):

> 'Currently, the vast majority of university language assessment is norm-referenced rather than criterion-referenced, and in the old universities it is heavily dependent on translation and general essay.'
> (Coleman and Rouxeville, in Coleman, 1997: 21)

Thirdly, a very high number of those older adult students, who already have some language learning experience, will have experienced traditional teaching as it was carried out in school years ago, i.e. grammar-centred, with little or even no emphasis at all on communication. As will be shown later, there was great reluctance among many adult learners to adopt a communicative approach in learning and be assessed in a language.

What constitutes communicative assessment?

At first, we have to define what we mean by teaching communicatively. Is it about enabling students just to pass on a message, no matter how distorted it becomes, as long as *'an extremely sympathetic native speaker is straining and managing to understand it'*, as one disgruntled and dismissive (former) part-time colleague put it?

This quote serves to illustrate a point: that the message about what constitutes the communicative teaching approach has been hopelessly jumbled and misunderstood by some tutors. This lamentable fact is partly due to tutors' lack of recent training or staff development, and partly due to the fact that providers are often too concerned with having a part-time tutor in front of the class, without checking that he or she possesses a sound understanding of appropriate methodology.

To understand the underlying principle of communicative teaching and assessment, the factors which contribute to the achievement of communicative competence have to be defined and understood. Communicative competence can be defined as the ability of the speaker/learner to draw upon four areas of knowledge:

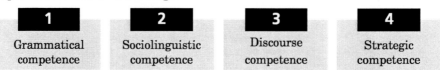

1	2	3	4
Grammatical competence	Sociolinguistic competence	Discourse competence	Strategic competence

(compare Canale and Swain, 1980)

However, these competencies refer to a knowledge **about** language, whereas communicative **performance** refers to the actual act of communication, using language as a native or non-native speaker.

A communicative performance can be achieved without an equal weighting in each of the competencies. As teachers we all, presumably, have come across students who excel in, for example, grammatical knowledge, but are tongue-tied when it comes to trying to speak to another person in the target language: they lack the knowledge in the other competence areas in order to perform satisfactorily. John Klapper (1997) points to this misconception of teaching and learning grammar in isolation:

> '*Grammar develops in the long term as a function of extensive exposure to , imitation and adaptation of the richest possible variety of language forms. The process can certainly be supported and indeed accelerated through conscious focusing on isolated grammatical forms allied to regular, targeted practice and re-enforcement , but it is only through freer, more creative and more contextualised activity that knowledge of grammatical forms can be transformed into habitual productive skills.*' (1997: 24)

He points to one of the important features of communicative assessment — the contextualisation of tasks. Assessment tasks should not only mirror tasks which reflect classroom practice, but they should also likewise mirror real-life tasks, as they might be encountered by students either in the target language culture or in the L1 culture, when they have to use their language skills. In order to do this, we have to take a closer look at the definition of communication.

> '*Communication' can be defined as:*
> * *interaction based;*
> * *unpredictable both in form and message;*
> * *varied according to sociolinguistic discourse contexts;*
> * *carried out under performance limitations (fatigue, memory, unfavourable environmental conditions;*
> * *always has a purpose;*
> * *involves authentic, as opposed to textbook contrived language;*
> * *judged to be successful or unsuccessful on the basis of actual outcomes.*'
> (Morrow, in Rivera, 1984: 39)

Therefore, if we claim to teach communicatively, our assessment tasks have to reflect these factors.

> '*If tests are to simulate reality, as closely as possible, recognition of the integrated nature of activities in certain contexts is necessary.*'
> (Weir, 1990: 84)

We have, therefore, adopted the notion of 'integrated tasks' into our assessment schemes. Although on certain occasions, tasks focusing on the practice of isolated skills are desirable and necessary for pedagogical reasons, assessment tasks should reflect the more complex situations in which communication takes place, which hardly ever require the application of just one skill and always serve a purpose.

This may serve as a brief introduction to the theoretical background. The issue of communicative assessment is discussed in more detail in another article (Hartley and Spöring, 1998).

Organisational background

Language classes are offered for members of the public through the Institute for Education and Lifelong Learning (IELL) and in 1997/98 offered five of sixteen languages on an accredited basis.[2] From the beginning, there had been collaboration and dovetailing with programmes with the mainstream Centre for Applied Language Studies (CALS) at the same institution. The following table gives an overview.

Language programmes at the University of Dundee 1997/98

	Description of course	Contact hours	Number of levels	Target group
Practical languages (IWLP)	Part of degree programme Full Credit	3 terms (3–5 hrs/week) approx. 84 hrs	6 stages (depending on entry qualification)	Undergraduate students
Open languages (IWLP)	1 year Half credit (20 SCOTCAT, level 1)	3 terms (2 hrs/week) 42 hrs	5 stages (4 stages accredited)	Students + staff
Languages in IELL (adult education)	1 year Half credit (20 SCOTCAT, level 1)	3 terms (2 hrs/week) 48 hours	5 stages (beginners to advanced) All accredited	Members of the public

Many tutors work in both Departments: IELL and CALS select and train tutors together. Both Departments also follow similar principles of teaching and assessment, adapted to their respective programmes and the needs of the learners.

As outlined in the following assessment timetable, the assessment system in IELL was designed to address the fears voiced by adult learners and to

---

2   Five stages per language, rated with 20 SCOTCAT points level 1, leading to a University Certificate in Modern Languages after completion of a one year course and assessment.

Institute for Education and Lifelong Learning _Certificate in Modern Languages_ Assessment format				
Continuous Assessment _Half of total mark_	**Term 1**	**Term 2**	**Term 3**	**Oral examination** _Half of total mark_
Stage 1 (introductory)	Listening	Writing/ Language structure	Speaking (to be assessed in class)	Duration: 10 mins Content: role play and picture based presentation and conversation
Stage 2 (lower intermediate)	Reading	Writing/ Language structure	Speaking/ listening (speaking to be assessed in class by tutor)	Duration: 10 mins Content: role play and general conversation based on stimulus
Stage 3 (intermediate)	Reading/ writing	Writing/ Language structure	Speaking/ listening (speaking to be assessed in class by tutor)	Duration: 15 mins Content: two more advanced role plays and discussion
Stage 4 (upper intermediate)	Reading/ writing	Writing/ Language Structure	Speaking (assessed presentation in class) Listening (assignment)	Duration: 15 mins Content: presentation/ talk (approx. 5 mins) on a chosen topic, discussion arising from this and other issues
Stage 5 (advanced)	Reading/ writing	Writing/ Language structure	Speaking (assessed presentation in class) Listening (assignment)	Duration: 20 mins Content: presentation/ talk (approx. 5 mins) on a chosen topic, discussion of general topic of interest arising from course

* Speaking assignments to be assessed in class, all other assignments to be done at home.

take account of their specific requirements and circumstances: studying in class for only two hours a week, and their need for guided, independent study at home, as some learners have to travel long distances.

As a result of market research carried out by the Institute, the curriculum and teaching methodology is communication-oriented, with a strong emphasis on oral communication. This fact is reflected in the stronger weighting given to oral communication: 50% for the final oral examination, as well as an oral assessment comprising one of the three continuous assessments carried out during the year.

Examples of contextualised communicative assessment tasks

As mentioned earlier, we have designed a framework of tasks deemed suitable for each stage of language learning. This can be used by tutors when designing their assessment tasks, supported by paper-setting guidelines. The assessments are checked against these guidelines, course descriptors and proficiency profiles for each language and stage by the Course Director for the programme. The accredited programme itself is also quality assured through a (CE based) external examiner, who is also a linguist.

An overview of the types of possible assessment tasks for the Beginners' and Advanced stages is given below:

Table for the analysis of assessment tasks
(based on a selection of tasks and stages)

Stage/level	Text type	Task type (see Key below*)	Skills used	Ques:Answ. L1? / L2?	Type of answer
Ab initio	Written instructions: role play	1,2,4	Read/speak/ listen	L2 : L2	Spoken: role play in pairs
Ab initio	Written instr. in L1, letter in L2	2,4,5	Read/write	L1 : L2	Written letter
Ab initio	Aural (3 mins.)	4	Listen/ write	L2 : L1	Written notes
ALL INTERMEDIATE STAGES OMITTED HERE					
Advanced	Written/ diagram	1,2,3,4,5,6,7	Read/write	L2 : L2 L2 : L1 L1 : L2	Written: letter/memo/ report/ article
Advanced	Aural (ca. 5 mins.)	2,3,4,6	Listen/write	L2 : L1 L2 : L2	Written in L1 or L2
Advanced	Written, visual, aural	1,2,3,4,5,6	Read/listen/ speak	L2 : L2 L1 : L2	Spoken

*Task types: key

1. problem-solving through social (face-to-face) interaction
2. establish/maintain relationship and discuss topics of interest through exchange of information/ideas/opinions
3. search for specific information — for given purpose; process it; and use.
4. listen to/ look at/ read information — process and use in some way
5. give information in spoken/written form on basis of personal experience
6. listen to/read/ view/ a story/poem/feature and respond to it personally
7. create an imaginative text

(Clark, 1987)

In order to illustrate this rather abstract table, we give examples here of continuous assessment tasks focusing on Beginners, Intermediate and Advanced stages. It should be borne in mind, however, that most tasks are easily adapted for different stages of language learning, depending on the type of material used and the task set.

| **A** | *A listening / writing task* |
| | *(Stage 2 / Lower Intermediate)* |

Audio text:	Authentic radio broadcast of approx. 3 minutes length.
Context:	Learner in L1 country.
Student instruction:	*You are listening to' – Radio X' and want to take part in their competition for language learners. You follow the broadcasters' instructions.*
Visual stimulus:	Postcard on answer sheet. The presenter in the programme is posing a number of questions such as: What is the capital of the (target language country)? Please tell us in one short sentence why you are learning the (target language)? The listener is then asked to send the postcard in to the station (address is given).
Task:	The student should complete a postcard in the target language, following entirely the instructions in the target language.

This task would be marked according to how successfully this has been achieved. At this stage the lack of accuracy is penalised only when meaning is impaired.

This kind of task would have to be adapted by the tutors of each target language to make it relevant to their culture. Not all countries have competitions for language learners, of course, nor are all countries in the grips of the National Lottery fever, etc.

Tasks have to be carefully adapted to suit the circumstances.

Another problem of course, is finding suitable material at the right time. This problem can only be addressed by constantly being on the lookout for material and building a bank of clippings, recordings and *realia* in general.

B *An oral assessment task (paired role play)*
(Stage 3 / Intermediate)

Student instruction: (in target language)
You are visiting your German friend during your trip to Germany. She works for the dole office in Hamburg and is talking to you about a case she is dealing with at work. She had been told by her boss to cut the unemployment benefit of a Hare Krishna supporter. He had refused to change his appearance for job interviews. You are discussing with your friend the legal and moral issues related to this case.

Again, this kind of task can only be set within a certain context. In this case, the class had been discussing moral issues surrounding personal freedom in conflict with demands of society, based on a unit in *Themen 2 (neu)*, dealing with unemployment, and a similar case of a punk with a Mohican haircut (*Themen neu 2, Lektion 1*).

Since the students had been dealing with a similar topic, they were prepared linguistically and emotionally to deal with this kind of issue. The moral stance the student takes is not important, but rather the ability to deal with a complex, potentially emotionally explosive situation.

C *A reading / writing / speaking task*
(Stage 5 / Advanced)

Text: City of Dundee information brochure, two pages containing general information about the area in English

Student instruction: *You are a member of the town twinning association (e.g. Dundee). You have been asked by the committee to welcome the next delegation from X at the reception organised for them. As you are the only person still keeping up your language skills through an evening class, they have asked you to prepare a brief presentation about the area.*

This task can be used in many ways. It can be used for a presentation in class, with other class members posing questions, inviting L2 speakers new to the area to the class, in a one-to-one situation for formal examination purposes. The task can focus on the writing aspect of it (prepare an information sheet for the visitors on an individual or group basis); it can be assessed informally by using it for the Twinning Association; or indeed it can be sent abroad to the respective L2 organisation for comment or to a similar group of language learners. It does not need to stand alone as an assessment task just for the sake of assessment only, it can form part of the normal learning taking place and be, therefore, not only of importance to the student(s) concerned, but the whole group, as it is serving a wider purpose.

D	*A reading / writing task*
	(Stage 5 / Advanced)

Text: Two articles taken from a Gaelic magazine and one of the regular articles in Gaelic in one of the main (English language!) dailies in Scotland on the issues surrounding the development of the Gaelic language.

Student instruction: *You have promised a friend of yours who works as a journalist in London and who knows only a little Gaelic that in your next letter you will summarise briefly the Gaelic articles he has found on the position of Gaelic speakers within Scotland.*

The student here is asked to write an informal text in L1, a situation which many language learners might be confronted with as a favour for friends or in a work context.

Great care in general has to be taken that the contexts and types of tasks provided do represent a wider range of themes, as set out in the course descriptors. In order to reflect the wide range of students and their interests within the classes, a number of factors has to be taken into account. Any one class may include students of a wide range of ages, retired, unemployed and employees in jobs ranging from manual to professional, people with different expectations, hoping to use the target language in social, leisure and/or work contexts.

Attitudes of learners

As described above, students have been reluctant initially to accept assessment, which they saw as imposed on them, despite them having a choice of opting into the scheme. There were strong feelings about the introduction of assessment when students' opinions were surveyed:

> *'The last thing I want is to go back to school where you are frightened about exams coming up. That's not something I want to put myself through!'*

> *'There might be some strife between students if one lot were really keen to study and do a lot of homework and other people were just there . . . .and the exam ones became more important than us.'*
> (Cooke, Mackle, and Spöring, 1996: 31)

Assessment was seen as something unnecessary for the process of learning:

> *'I don't see any reason to do it. It doesn't gee me up particularly. If I am going to gee myself up then I will.'* (ibid: 30)

> *'I think it would be a very good thing . . . to give me some incentive. . .'*
> (ibid: 32)

There is a stark difference in opinion between classes where assessment had been introduced already and those who had not yet experienced it.

> *'I think there is no difference, in fact until the people who were taking the Certificate identified themselves last week when they were taking the class, I don't think any of us had a clue who was taking the Certificate and who was not. The class is really working as it has always done'.* (ibid:33)

Since this survey was carried out in 1995–96, we have no data showing that the students are dissatisfied with the assessment. On the contrary, The Secretary of the Extramural Students Association expressed the view that assessment had not impeded students' satisfaction.

Tutors' attitudes to assessment

The majority of tutors were open and positive about the fact that formalised assessment had been introduced into the courses. Apart from one tutor, who felt challenged in his professional practice and chose to leave, rather than to adapt and change, all tutors welcomed the fact that there were now regular staff development sessions for them, which focused on specific issues as well as general guidelines which detailed learning outcomes for each language learning stage. Some examples of our tutor survey, carried out in 1996, may serve to illustrate the point that the introduction of assessment was seen as positive. All tutors surveyed confirmed that they saw the introduction of assessment as mainly positive. A selection of tutors' responses follows (based on the IELL/CALS language tutors' survey in 1996):

> *'Students who choose to do the assessment take the course more seriously, learn more and appreciate what they do better.'*

> *'The format of the assessments is enjoyable.'*

> *'Assessments are generally imaginative and enjoyable, even while being challenging.'*

> *'They provide an opportunity to measure progress and identify limits. They can also be a source of reassurance.'*

> *'Having finished my first year, my second year of teaching will be more assessment-orientated simply in terms of preparing all students for particular types of task or exercise: this is the main way my teaching has been influenced this year, too . . .'*

> *'There is such a sense of achievement after going through all the stages of the certificate. I would like to see many more students doing it.'*

> *'I enjoy preparing the assessments. It is more challenging for all'*

In general, although tutors seemed to welcome warmly the introduction of assessments, many of them mentioned that they had to change their teaching and class room management; which they saw in a positive light. Only one tutor was concerned about having to teach assessed and non-assessed students together, without giving any reasons.

Conclusion

Student and tutor feedback has shown that contextualised communicative assessment tasks can work, without having a negative impact on students' and tutors' morale. It can, on the contrary, increase the quality of learning, as tutor and student focus more on tasks, which are seen as purposeful and applicable to real-life situations. It has a positive backwash effect on the teaching and learning situation. Assessment is not necessarily seen any more as a separate, fear-inducing process reminiscent of past and often negative learning experiences. The fact that those opting into the scheme (for a separate fee) has increased in IELL from 19 % to 30% over four academic years points to a general acceptance of the scheme. It is envisaged that the numbers of students opting in will increase considerably when the assessment fee is waived in the 1998/99 session.

Despite all its shortcomings and problems, we were pleasantly surprised at the positive outcome of the evaluation of the accredited language programme. This was despite the many difficulties experienced in regards to standardisation, staff development, administration and organisation.[3]

We have so far tried to juggle an array of balls in the air, at the same time striving:

- to give all students a good learning experience;
- to give a qualification to those students wishing to obtain one;
- to give tutors better teaching support and staff development opportunities;
- to provide high quality language tuition to the wider community, as referred to in the University's mission statement;
- to comply with the HE Funding Council requirements.

However, we are only too aware of the fact that we have to operate under increasing financial pressures. Trying to keep everyone happy is no easy task!

---

1   This is the reason for the gradual introduction of more languages to the scheme; In 1998–99 a further four languages are to come on stream as accredited courses.

Bibliography

Aufderstrasse H and H E Piepho, *Themen 2 (neu)*, Kursbuch (Germany: Hueber Verlag, 1984)

Canale M and M Swain, 'Theoretical bases of communicative approaches to second language teaching and testing' in *Journal of Applied Linguistics* (Vol 1, No. 1, 1980)

Clark J, *Curriculum renewal in school foreign language learning* (OUP, 1987)

Coleman J A, *Studying languages. A survey of British and European students. The proficiency, background, attitudes and motivations of students of foreign languages in the UK and Europe* (CILT, 1997)

Cooke A, K Mackle and M Spöring, 'Sleeping at the back. Student attitudes to accreditation' in *Scottish Journal of Adult and Continuing Education* (1996)

Hartley L and M Spöring, 'Teaching communicatively: assessing communicatively?' in *Language Learning Journal* (ALL, 1998)

Hawkins E (ed), *30 years of language teaching* (CILT, 1996)

Klapper J, 'Language learning at school and at university: the great grammar debate continues (1)' in *Language Learning Journal* (ALL, 1997)

Rivera C (ed), *Communicative competence approaches to language proficiency assessment: research and application* (Multilingual Matters, 1984)

Weir C J, 'Communicative language testing' in *Exeter Linguistics Studies No.11* (Prentice-Hall International, 1988, reprinted 1990)

Assessment and accreditation of languages: implications for tutor training

7

Anke Hübner, University of Nottingham

The new funding criteria as outlined in the circular of the Higher Education Funding Council for England (HEFCE) have resulted in university departments of higher education having to offer accredited courses in order to attract funding.

> *'In 1995–96 and beyond, continuing education provision which results in a recognised HE award, and also that continuing education which is accredited and can contribute to an HE award (or is credit-bearing within a credit accumulation framework), will be eligible for funding.'* (HEFCE Circular 3/94)

Funding depends on decisions made by government and educational institutions have to adapt accordingly. David Minton explains this fact to future adult educators:

> *'Assessment is an important process, one which is taken seriously by learners and teachers alike. You will be aware that it is also of interest to the Government, which regularly intervenes in the way in which the achievements of both school-children and adults are assessed. It devises policies and sets up bodies to regulate assessment according to currently held beliefs about learning and achievement'.* (Minton, 1997: 196)

The question of accreditation and assessment is therefore of extreme importance.

The approaches taken and difficulties encountered by part-time tutors when assessing adult language learners are described and analysed in this article. The focus will be on the implications for future tutor training based on the findings.

Practical material

The practical material is drawn from the extra-mural language programmes 1995/96 and 1996/97 of the department of continuing education, Nottingham University. Each academic year comprised approximately 100 modern foreign language courses covering ten different modern foreign languages at five stages taught by some 40 hourly-paid part-time tutors. Courses are held in the University adult education centre in Nottingham as well as in centres in Derby and Matlock (Derbyshire), Lincoln and Boston (Lincolnshire) and more isolated rural areas.

The material is collected from the following three sources:

- **samples of work** done in the 1995/96 and 1996/97 assessment rounds. The internal monitoring was carried out and recorded by the author in her role as language course director;

- **personal statement of learning forms** of the academic years 1995/96 and 1996/97 (PSL). These forms accompany each course syllabus and are designed specifically for the department of continuing education at Nottingham University. The forms are filled out by students at the end of the course. PSLs can be seen as students' self assessment as well as a course evaluation. We aim for a 100% return rate of PSLs per course because completed forms count as proof of students' participation and are therefore crucial for funding;

- **tutor report forms** of the academic years 1995/96 and 1996/97.

In order to receive remuneration, each tutor has to fill out one form per course. Both the PSL form and the tutor report form are included in the tutor handbook which is distributed to each tutor before the start of the course. (See Appendix 3, p118, for a completed PSL form.)

This article draws upon a multitude of quotations taken from PSLs and tutor report forms and offers samples of assignments where appropriate in order to develop a list of assessment principles suitable for assessing the adult language learner. These principles will form the basis for the design of a tutor training module as part of a higher education qualification for part-time tutors teaching modern foreign languages to adults.

Tutors' and students' perceptions of accreditation and assessment (as revealed in the practical material)

Susan Ainslie forecasts in her article *'Testing language performance'*:

> *'The initial reaction of adult education tutors and students alike to the suggestion that they are working towards some form of accreditation can be hostile, to say the least. Adults don't like being tested; adult education is about leisure and pleasure, so why put the*

students through the ordeal of being tested?; the vast majority of adult students have no need or use for any sort of qualification. The terror on the face of the enrolling beginner on being told that the course leads to some sort of a test confirms the teacher in this view. And at enrolment, if you would like the student to come to the first lesson, let alone the rest of the course, it would be a good idea to say that the test is entirely optional!' (Ainslie in Arthur and Hurd, 1993: 127)

It should be noted that in 1993 the words *testing* and *test* were probably more acceptable than today.

In order to assess tutors' perceptions of the introduction of assessment, 200 tutor report forms filled in by language tutors working for the department of continuing education at Nottingham University were examined. It was expected that the quality of the assignments might depend on the tutors' reactions to the changes. Surprisingly, only one tutor report form revealed concerns about the assignments:

'We decided to base each assignment upon a different topic (getting around / shopping / eating out / booking accommodation). Students who were complete beginners were quite concerned about those assignments but their results are encouraging and are a good reflection of their efforts made throughout the course.' (Tutor report French Stage 1, Term 1, 1996/97, Nottingham)

However, only one student out of nine from this particular language course commented in the PSL form on the assignments as follows:

'There is too much assessment for such a short course [. . .]. These courses are not credited — I feel that much time was spent unnecessarily — who really wants to check or waste time on these — you!' (PSL, French Stage 1, Term 1, 1996/97, Nottingham)

One student on a more advanced course mentioned in the PSL form that she had to be persuaded to hand in work for assessment:

'I have had to buckle down to producing work to be marked. The course has kept my mind alert . . . ' (PSL, French Stage 4, Year 2, 1996/97, Matlock)

Apart from these few examples, no further positive or negative comments related to assessment were found in PSL forms. It can therefore be concluded that on the whole neither language tutors nor students at Nottingham University were opposed to assessment and accreditation. The report *'All Change! Accreditation as a Challenge to Liberal Adult Education'*, carried out at the centre for continuing education at the University of Sussex, came to the same conclusion:

'On the whole departments seemed to think that existing students were not disposed towards accreditation.' (Ambrose, Holloway, Mayhew, 1994: 45)

However, most of the 26 continuing education departments which took part in the Sussex research thought that:

> 'Careful marketing and low key assessment will present accreditation in a positive light.' (Ambrose, Holloway and Mayhew, 1994: Summary)

Introduction of accreditation and assessment at the department of continuing education, Nottingham University

Nottingham University's approach towards the introduction of accreditation focused on low key assessment and careful explanation of accreditation as solutions:

> 'Our certificated courses are already popular and recruit extremely well. Staff have been discussing accreditation informally with students and many seemed prepared to accept accreditation especially if it kept the cost of courses down! At a formal level, we intend to explain carefully to students the definitions of assessment and accreditation once we know the intentions of the HEFCE. Many students think that assessment means exams and are relieved to discover that it isn't so daunting. Also some appreciate the formalisation of their educational development even if they are not looking for pathways into HE.' (Ambrose, Holloway and Mayhew, 1994: 48)

Introduction of accreditation and assessment for modern language courses at the department of continuing education, Nottingham University

Following the principle of low key assessment, a succession of tutor training meetings in the academic years 1995/96 and 1996/97 were used to carefully explain the need for assessment and accreditation of language courses and to gently implement general assessment guidelines for the different types of courses offered at the department of continuing education at Nottingham University:

- in **language courses** all four linguistic skills should be assessed continuously, i.e. formative assessment should be implemented.

The German continuing education institution *Volkshochschule (VHS)* has introduced the same guidelines and emphasises the assessment of the four linguistic skills in their *VHS* certificates:

> '*Die Zertifikats-Lernziele sind vor allem auf die praktische Verwertbarkeit des Gelernten ausgerichtet, auf Verständigung in Situationen des täglichen Lebens. Daher wird auf der einen Seite die Ausbildung der vier Grundfertigkeiten beschrieben: Hören, Sprechen, Lesen, Schreiben. Auf der anderen Seite stehen inhaltliche bzw. kommunikative Lernziele [. . .]*' . (Bianchi, Busch and Sommet, 1987: 30)

- for **conversation classes** only the skill of speaking should be assessed continuously;

- for more **advanced language courses and literature courses** taught through the target language, the fifth skill of translating might be assessed, depending on the length of the course either in addition to the other linguistic skill areas or to replace one of the other four skills;

- **language, society and culture courses** have the main learning objective to heighten cultural awareness and are targeted at non-linguists. These courses have a minimal language input and the society and culture component is taught in English. For these courses there is no need to assess linguistic skills.

General principles of good assessment practice

For the integration of assessment into teaching and learning the following principles for good practice were agreed upon by the course directors and their teams of part-time tutors:

- the **purposes of assessment** need to be clear;

- assessment should be an **integral part** of the teaching and learning, therefore **continuous assessment** should be implemented;

- the function of assessment should be **formative and diagnostic** of progress and strengths and weaknesses, i.e. it should be a means of delivering feedback to learner and tutor during the course;

- assessment in adult education has to be **criterion referenced** nowadays, i.e. the learner's performance is measured against a set of agreed criteria, that is according to the learning objectives ('*Lernziele*') of the course which feature in the course syllabus and are repeated as learning outcomes in the PSL forms (see Appendix 4, p120, for a sample of a course syllabus). If everyone has achieved the objectives, i.e. is able to fulfil the criteria, then there is a pass rate of 100%. The German *VHS-Verband* speaks of '*Lernerfolgskontrolle*' (control of successful learning) using a new term with a positive connotation instead of calling it *Prüfung* (examination):

'*Durch Lernerfolgskontrollen kann festgestellt werden, inwieweit die gesetzten Lernziele erreicht werden. [. . .] Lernerfolgskontrollen sind nicht allein mit Sprachtests gleichzusetzen.*' (Bianchi, Busch and Sommet, 1987: 102);

- the assessment methodology should aim to **be valid**, i.e. it should assess what it sets out to assess;

- assessment should aim to **be reliable**, i.e. it should produce a similar spread of results if given again to a similar group of learners. The most reliable tasks are those where questions have only one correct answer, for example multiple choice tests.

Back to the Nottingham case: since assessment methods and materials should be linked closely to the teaching, it was not deemed appropriate to develop a rigid and structured assessment scheme as far as the type of assessment activity, the assessment method, and materials were concerned.

In order to achieve low key assessment and to respect the pedagogical freedom of the tutor and the diverse requirements of specific courses, it was left to the individual tutor to design his or her own assessment tasks and administer the assessment for his or her course. Ainslie and Lamping have devoted a whole book to the topic '*Assessing adult learners*'. They point out that:

'*There is no single correct way to go about assessment, and there is a variety of techniques which could be used. All of these can be suitable for certain learners in certain circumstances, but it is important to remember that any technique selected should allow learners to use the kind of language they would actually us in 'real' situations. There seems little justification for including in adult classes today techniques such as reading aloud a prepared passage. Tutors must choose techniques which best answer their learners' needs.*' (Ainslie and Lamping, 1995: 25)

The principles of linguistic assessment: practical examples of assessment tasks and students' and tutors' perceptions thereof

The monitoring of the assessment rounds of the academic years 1995/96 and 1996/97 resulted in the compilation of examples of laudable as well as less praiseworthy assessment tasks. The shortcomings in the design of assignments and in the execution of assessment indicates that the majority of language tutors — especially tutors who come from the liberal adult education background — are not used to assessment duties. There is clearly a need for tutor training in that field.

The following assessment principles are listed in order of their occurrence in PSL or tutor report forms. The quotes taken from these forms are then supported by practical examples of assessment tasks as appropriate. For Principles 11, 12, and 13 no quotes from tutors or students could be found as these principles were mainly ignored by tutors or are simply not implemented to date.

> ### Assessment Principle 1
> Assessment tasks should be **relevant to adult life** and have **real-life value**.

Everyday experiences, world knowledge, and the interests and needs of the adult learner have to be central in the communicative learner-centred teaching of today. Bianchi, Busch and Sommet acknowledge this and point out the challenge this presents to tutor and learner alike:

> 'Alltag, Erfahrungsbereich und Interessen des Lernenden sollen zunehmend eine größere Rolle im Lernprozess spielen. Dies stellt an nicht wenige Kursleiter und Teilnehmer neue Forderungen. Sie müssen gemeinsam — also partnerschaftlich — die Brücke schlagen zwischen abstrakt formulierten Lernzielen und dem persönlichen Leben des einzelnen.' (Bianchi, Busch and Sommet, 1987: 31)

This is an area where the shortcomings of textbooks become obvious as the number of good modern language textbooks aimed at the adult learner market is still rather limited. However, ideas for adult specific assessment materials and methods can easily be adapted from materials produced for teaching English as a foreign language which historically has a wider teaching resource base.

Students welcome the use of a variety of stimulating authentic text types, e.g. texts in the broad sense which include everything containing words such as stickers, advertisements, labels:

> 'Because this French course does not rely on the use of a textbook, but on input from the tutor, it is able to satisfy the needs of the students and continues to remain stimulating and interesting.' (PSL, French Stage 2, Year 2, 1996/97, Nottingham)

For example, the ideal material for assessing the competence of exchanging information about the housing market in the country of the target language could be an authentic property guide. It is highly likely that native speaker tutors will have fewer problems finding authentic materials. The above mentioned French class, for instance, was taught by a tutor who is married to a French lady and has a property in France.

Closely linked to relevance to adult life is the principle of real-life value. Assessment tasks should simulate situations which may happen when travelling or meeting native speakers of the target language. Most adult learners comment on real-life value when filling out the PSL forms. They focus on everyday situations which they might encounter in the near future. The following comments underpin the main learning outcome and give an indication of why people opt to learn a foreign language in adult life:

> 'Continuing the course in the Spring term and then trying it out on the locals when I visit France later this year!' (PSL, French Stage 2, Year 2, Term 1, 1996/97, Nottingham)

> 'I won't feel quite so ignorant or self-conscious next time I visit friends in Spain. [...] I feel much more able to communicate both verbally and in writing with Spanish friends. [...] .' (PSL, Spanish language, life and culture, Term 1, 1996/97, Cotgrave)

> '[...] the language in relation to a 'holiday' situation. [...] Key situations, e.g. shopping, bank, etc.' (PSL, Italian Stage 2, Year 1, 1996/97, Matlock)

> 'I visit France each year and am closely connected with twinning with Orgain in the Loire Valley. I feel this course has helped me to understand French spoken at a normal speed and to communicate with French friends.' (PSL, French Stage 4, Year 2, 1996/97, Matlock)

Real-life value of assessment tasks could be enhanced by the use of authentic up-to-date material. For example, an authentic menu imported from the target country is better than a menu handwritten or word processed by the tutor. Students clearly recognise the extra value of authentic materials provided by the native speaker tutor:

> 'The lessons in this course are what I have been waiting for! There is no substitute for being taught by a native speaker [...]. The lessons are lively, amusing and stimulating using a wide variety of materials from [authentic] magazine articles to videotapes of [authentic] news, advertisement and even the presidential address on New Year's Eve. My vocabulary has been enlarged and my understanding of idiomatic Italian improved.' (PSL, Italian conversation Stage 4, Year 1, 1996/97, Matlock)

The following selection of activities could be described as preferable to ready made textbook activities because they have the additional factor of authenticity:

	▼ Competence to be assessed	▼ Materials
Example A	Identifying a route	Recording on audiotape Authentic map
Example B	Requesting information about houses for sale in a selected region/town of the target country	Individual or group letter to foreign estate agents
Example C	Requesting information about adult education classes abroad	Questionnaire to adult education providers in the target country.

Assessment activities where the learner takes on the role of the waiter or waitress in a restaurant or the receptionist in a hotel or a telephone operator might well be relevant for undergraduates preparing their work placements abroad, but not for adult learners who will most certainly be at the receiving end of the above mentioned communicative situations when travelling abroad. If the role of the waiter, shop assistant or bank clerk has to be filled, it should probably be performed by the tutor.

In order to achieve real-life value, assessment tasks ought to be fully contextualised, i.e. the situation should be set in a realistic context. Examples for contextualisation are text manipulation tasks where an authentic newspaper article is transformed into a radio commentary to be broadcasted by a foreign radio station.

Another example of a contextualised assessment task is quoted under assessment Principle 3. In this case the listening task is combined with the task of note-taking in the target language:

> 'You are staying at a friend's flat in Paris. He has asked you to check the messages on his answerphone and to ring him at work. He is particularly anxious to know about his car which he has left for repairs at a local garage. You listen to the message and note down: [...]'. (see Appendices 6 and 7, French Stage 1, 1996/97, Nottingham)

Assessment Principle 2

Assessment should be carried out in a **relaxed and friendly** atmosphere.

Creating a relaxed and friendly atmosphere is crucial when integrating assessment into teaching and learning. Ainslie and Lamping point out that all depends on the sympathetic tutor:

> 'The atmosphere of the adult classroom is generally relaxed. Discipline is not an issue and there need be no distance between tutor and learners. [...] The tutor's most important task when setting up assessment is to maintain this relaxed atmosphere. If this is not done, and the classroom is allowed to become stressful, it is unlikely that assessment will be as effective as it should be, as it is unlikely to properly reflect learners' competence.' (Ainslie and Lamping, 1995: 21–22)

Not surprisingly, the importance of a relaxed atmosphere was pointed out quite regularly by adult learners.

Here are a few general comments taken from a variety of PSL forms:

> 'It was a pleasant relaxed atmosphere and therefore easy to learn in [...] enjoyed the informal way the lessons were conducted. [...]
>
> Relaxed atmosphere encourages contributions in class.' (PSL, French Stage 2, Year 2, Term 1, 1996/97, Nottingham)

'[...] relaxing and enjoyable but firmly led [...] The tutor has a warm, friendly personality [...].' (PSL, German Stage 1, Term 1, 1996/97, Nottingham)

An example of how assessment should not be executed was recorded in a rural adult education centre where students had to wait in the corridor outside the classroom for their turn to perform in front of a microphone. (German Stage 3, Term 1, 1996/97, Boston)

However, the use of the microphone is indispensable as there needs to be proof of learning if credits are to be awarded for the successful completion of an adult education course. Tape recordings done by students at home are for example the basis for the speaking assessment in all Open University language courses.

But it goes without saying that:

> *'Many adults become anxious and tongue tied when required to 'perform' in front of an audience, or into a microphone. A speaking test involving the learner in a one-to-one interview can produce a totally unacceptable discrepancy between the competence he or she actually demonstrates and the competence we know he or she could demonstrate in different circumstances. This is especially true of those adults who are not driven to learn a language primarily to gain qualifications.'* (Ainslie and Lamping, 1995: 23)

Unfortunately, today's government's funding requirements do not allow for liberal adult education without assessment and accreditation. Therefore the only solution to avoid stress and anxiety related to assessment activities is to make assessment part of the teaching and learning process. In the case of speaking activities this means that if learners are used to seeing and using microphones and tape recorders right from the start of the language course as essential and beneficial tools, there is no reason why they should not also be used throughout an assessment activity. To add some element of choice and realism to the exercise, students should be allowed to choose the topic, for example leaving a message in the target language on an answering machine or enquiring on the telephone about the availability and prices of hotel rooms. They should get used to performing a variety of tasks regularly at home or with fellow students during the session enabling them to select one recorded performance for assessment. A Japanese class where six role play situations were offered on role play cards so that students could choose and get familiar with the tasks set can be seen as a favourable example.

A good way to avoid stress building up during the session is to opt for two or more learners to take part in a discussion or role play on a given topic while the rest of the group is engaged in other linguistic activities. But generally speaking, co-operation between students is very much welcomed by adult learners:

'*A friendly co-operative group where we all help each other. Much of the credit for this goes to [the tutor] who leads us along with a minimum of formality and fuss.*' (PSL, Italian Stage 2, Year 2, Term 1, 1996/97, Nottingham)

The tutor of the same course comments on his or her successful implementation of audio recordings in and out of the classroom:

'*We have also recorded some of our work (despite temporary problems with equipment at one time in Oct / Nov) + individual students have recorded themselves at home.*' (Tutor report, Italian Stage 2, Year 2, Term 1, 1996/97, Nottingham)

Assessment Principle 3

Assessment should be an integral part of the learning process and therefore continuous in nature, i.e. it should not be carried out under exam type conditions at the end of the course.

It is noticeable that students recognise a '*sense of achievement*' through continuous assessment and welcome constructive and prompt feedback as the following quotes show:

'*The continuing support shows the success of the tutor in giving students a sense of achievement. There is no sense of pressure, yet a steady rate of progress is achieved.*' (PSL, Italian Stage 2, Year 2, Term 1, 1996/97, Nottingham)

'*Constant changes of activity keep us very much on the alert, and each lesson leaves me with a sense of achievement.*' (PSL, Italian conversation, Stage 4, Year 1, Term 1, 1996/97, Matlock)

'*Written work has been encouraged and marked (with helpful comments) promptly.*' (PSL, Italian Stage 1, Term 1, 1996/97, Nottingham)

However, one disappointed student who would have liked more work comments.

'*I'm sorry to say that I have been disappointed in this course. To put it simply, we haven't been worked hard enough especially as far as homework (particularly marked homework) is concerned. [...]*

I would have welcomed more structured learning, and more rigour in commenting on students' contributions to the class — not everything we do is 'stupendo'!' (PSL, Spanish Stage 2, Year 2, 1996/97, Matlock)

Integrated assessment has recently been introduced by the Open University for their second Year of the German course *L230 Motive: Moving on in German*. From February 1998 the following applies:

'*[...] listening, reading and writing are not assessed separately. In the TMAs [Teacher Marked Assignments] there are writing assignments, in which students read and/or listen to material before writing on the same subject, and there are speaking assignments in which students read and/or listen to material before speaking on the same subject.'* (The Open University, 1997:6)

Integrated assessment proves not only less time consuming but also more natural as every conversation activates listening and speaking ability simultaneously. A practical example of integrated assessment was found in a French beginners course where the role play *'Au garage'* was reinforced by a listening comprehension exercise based on a ficticious answerphone message *'Note taking of costs for car repair'*.

Well perceived by students are classes which offer a mix of linguistic activities, some done during the session and others to be done at home:

'The lessons are very enjoyable — we are kept busy with tasks varying all the time. The homework set is always checked.' (PSL, Italian Stage 1, Term 1, 1996/97, Nottingham)

While making homework or take away exercises (as they are called at the University of Dundee, Centre for continuing education) an integral part of the course, some tutors switch to distance learning mode which is necessary to keep the momentum going because contact hours of adult education classes are mostly restrained to 1.5 or 2 hours per week. However, take away exercises might result in more work for the tutor:

'As in previous years there has been a constant flow of written work handed in for correction ... ' (Tutor report, Italian Stage 2, Year 2, Term 1, 1996/97, Nottingham)

Assessment Principle 4

Assessment should be **challenging**.

Tutors and students alike favoured a challenge. The quotations speak for themselves. *'Varied exercises'* and *'kept on our toes'* were mentioned regularly:

'[The tutor] used an excellent range of activities, and was very creative in their use, to allow us to experience and reinforce learning points.' (PSL, Spanish Stage 1, 1996/97, Nottingham)

'Excellent course [...] varied exercises, in quick succession. We are kept on our toes, work hard and quickly. But it's very enjoyable, too. [...] We never get soft options, and this is good!' (PSL, Italian conversation Stage 4, Year 1, Term 1, 1996/97, Matlock)

'Excellent course, well structured, stimulating and interesting. Very pleasant atmosphere. We are kept on our toes!' (PSL, French Stage 2, Year 2, Term 1, 1996/97, Nottingham)

And the tutor of the same course was delighted:

> *'Students commented that the course was stimulating, interesting and well-structured. [. . .] We are kept on our toes — was one of the comments which pleased me the most!'* (Tutor report, French Stage 2, Year 2, Term 1, 1996/97, Nottingham)

Assessment Principle 5

Development of **all four/five linguistic skills** (depending on the nature of the course as outlined under point 5).

Adult learners are conscious of the learning process and the fact that all linguistic skills are developed in a course was commented upon favourably:

> *'This course has enabled me to continue practising the [. . .] language (reading, writing, speaking and listening) and at the same time increasing my vocabulary and usage of past and future tenses — all in real-life situations.'* (PSL, French Stage 2, Year 2, Term 1, 1996/97, Nottingham)

Some students are well aware of the main objective of a modern language course which should be the development of the skill of speaking, especially if the course is called *'Get by in Italian'* or *'French for travellers'*:

> *'I have thoroughly enjoyed the course but would welcome more opportunity to speak Italian.'* (PSL, Italian Stage 1, Term 1, 1996/97, Nottingham)

Assessment Principle 6

Listening comprehension tasks should include a **variety of authentic native speaker voices** — male and female — at natural speed and in authentic settings, e.g. with background noises where appropriate.

Learners are often exposed exclusively to their tutor's voice during contact hours. An additional input via audiocassette containing authentic male and female voices could be beneficial. Inviting native speaker guests to the class is a wonderful idea, too, but demands some planning and of course access to native speakers. One student expresses unhappiness with his or her listening performance. The cause for this might be the result of insufficient practice or age-related hearing problems or the bad quality of recordings or record players used for listening comprehension tasks. The latter is well possible since comments on bad quality of equipment are made by students and tutors, especially when classes are taught in rural areas where accommodation is often less than ideal and no teaching aids are available:

> *'I can understand [the tutor], but have problems with audio tapes. I watch whatever TV I can, though cable has taken off Rai Uno. English TV sometimes has Italian.'* (PSL, Italian Stage 2, Year 2, Term 1, 1996/97, Nottingham)

Occasionally, tutors encourage students to take advantage of self-access materials provided by the institution in order to develop the skill of listening:

> 'Four students regularly used the Language Laboratory — mainly to watch the news or a documentary programme in the evening.' (Tutor report, French Stage 2, Year 2, Term 1, 1996/97, Nottingham)

▌**Assessment Principle 7**

▌Assessment activities should have a **grammar** component.

Adult students are conscious language learners, in need of explanations and grammatical rules. Very often they studied a language years ago at school and they are used to a non-communicative language learning method. The needs resulting from this should be taken into consideration when teaching foreign languages to adults. Sometimes the foreign language learning experience from school leaves adults with unpleasant memories. This seems to apply to adult language learners of all nationalities as the following German quotation indicates:

> 'Die ungewohnte Situation des 'Zurück auf die Schulbank' ist im Reflex lange zurückliegender, aber internalisierter Lernerfahrungen zu sehen; in diesem Kontext wurzelnde Lerntraditionen sollten daher Berücksichtigung finden. Die ungewohnte psycho-soziale Situation, die die Schülerrolle im Alter zur Folge hat, kann zu vielfältigen Unsicherheiten führen, die von regredierenden Tendenzen bis zu Lernblockaden aus Versagensangst reichen. Der ältere Lerner zeigt eine starke Tendenz zur Selbstkritik, oftmals verbunden mit einem ungerechtfertigt negativen Selbstkonzept und einer daraus resultierenden niedrigen Frustrationsschwelle.' (Berndt, 1997: 73)

The fact that relevance to adult life and the need for a relaxed and friendly learning environment featured high in students' opinions (see Assessment Principles 1 and 2) supports Berndt's view of adult learners' low self-esteem (*'negativen Selbstkonzept'*), tendency to self-criticism (*'starke Tendenz zur Selbstkritik'*) and low threshold of frustration (*'niedrigen Frustrations- schwelle'*).

Students used to a grammatical approach very often complain about the lack of grammar in modern language teaching:

> 'I would have liked more direct teaching on grammar, clauses, verb tenses etc., to expand my knowledge in a more progressive way.' (PSL, Welsh Stage 3, Year 1, Term 1, 1996/97, Nottingham)

Some positive interactive examples of grammar assessment in a non-traditional way were observed in a number of language classes. Practising prepositions in a playful stimulating way using authentic objects hidden in different places of the room is one example. This kind of interactive task was referred to by the following student when she wrote:

> '[The tutor] uses class situations to bring up grammatical points and vocabulary which are relevant.' (PSL, French Stage 2, Year 2, Term 1, 1996/97, Nottingham)

Another interesting example is a giant town map designed by the tutor which is put on the floor of the teaching room. One student has the task to give directions in the target language for the assessment of speaking skills, a second student had to walk on the map, i.e. carry out the directions which assessed the listening skill. The rest of the group watched in amazement while being entertained. Everybody participated in the listening task by observing the fellow students' performance.

Assessment Principle 8

Assessment should offer **differentiated tasks** in order to cater for mixed-ability, mixed-experience, mixed-expectation learner groups.

Adult language classes demand differentiated learning modes and differentiated tasks for fair assessment. Convery and Coyle focus on language learning at school but their flexible approach is just as valid for adult language learning:

> '[...] there is a variety of ways in which differentiation can be achieved [...] by text [...] by interest [...] by task'. (Convery and Coyle, 1993: 3–5)

In order to assess reading comprehension for example, learners

> 'may be working on the same text, but the tasks they are required to do can be graded in difficulty and matched to differing needs and abilities.' (Convery and Coyle, 1993: 5)

This would certainly mean more preparation for the tutor, but it would be student-centred and do justice to adults' differing needs.

Only a few examples of differentiation were recorded in Nottingham but students do seem to recognise its value:

> 'The style of teaching methods and encouragement have enabled me to join in at my own level, i.e. role play, group work, pair work, games.' (PSL, Italian Stage 2, Year 1, 1996/97, Matlock)

And in the eyes of a tutor:

> 'Some students attempted more difficult assignments e.g. difficult translations. Others attempted easier passages, but overall the results were good and a high standard was generally achieved.' (Tutor report, Welsh Stage 3, Year 1, Term 1, 1996/97)

> ### Assessment Principle 9
> Assessment activities should be accompanied by well-presented **support material**.

In both assessment rounds there was a lack of support material such as handouts, worksheets or cue cards. Sometimes, little handwritten paper slips were handed out to students offering minimal help such as topic-related vocabulary. Ideally, tutors should provide word processed handouts and worksheets with ample space for learners to make notes.

Students value additional material as was pointed out in one PSL:

> *'Audio-visual aids were also used on a regular basis and a constant supply of handouts was made available. The latter provided us with an insight at contemporary Italian life.'* (PSL, Italian conversation Stage 4, Year 1, 1996/97, Matlock)

> ### Assessment Principle 10
> Assessment activities should be reinforced by constructive encouraging **feedback**.

The value of feedback on work done by students was touched on earlier when students commented positively on feedback or correction of homework. Monitoring of assignments showed that there exists a lack of feedback forms or assignment comment forms as they are sometimes called. As Race and Brown state:

> *'Feedback to learners is probably the most crucial ingredient in any recipe for successful learning.'* (Race and Brown, 1995: 56)

In that context it comes as a surprise that the only traces of feedback came in form of one or two short sentences scribbled by tutors under students' written work, sometimes encouraging words like *'well done'* were added. Most feedback messages were written in English — this applies to beginners as well as to more advanced classes. Only occasionally, did tutors use single encouraging words in the target language.

Everybody needs feedback to feel positive about achievement.

Rather discouraging for students is the use of red ink in written work, a habit Race/Brown invite tutors to think about:

> *'Think about the effect red ink has on learners. Even when an excellent essay or report is returned covered with red comments (however positive) there is an instinctive anxiety on seeing 'all the red' on the script. This anxiety can get in the way of receiving feedback in a calm, objective way.'* (Race and Brown, 1993: 90)

In spite of that, one student of an advanced French class used the PSL form to express his or her opinion on marking, correction and usefulness of feedback:

> 'All our written homework was marked and corrected as necessary and useful notes added.' (PSL, French Stage 2, Year 2, Term 1, 1996/97, Matlock)

Another shortcoming revealed by the monitoring of the assessment rounds is the fact that no feedback at all was given on the assessment of speaking. This should ideally be done straight after the speaking task is carried out or in the case of recordings done at home there should be a constructive feedback message by the tutor recorded on the same audiotape. At lower stages these messages should be in English, whereas at intermediate and more advanced level the target language could be used to give constructive feedback.

Feedback on oral work was attempted by only one tutor who wrote a feedback message, pointing out incorrect genders and tenses, but unfortunately did not mention intonation and pronunciation. (French Stage 4, Year 2, Term 1, 1996/97, Matlock)

Race and Brown devote in their book an entire chapter to 'Giving learners verbal feedback'. This chapter gives much food for thought. (Race and Brown, 1993: 90)

As a first step towards heightening tutors' awareness of the importance of feedback, checklists for both written feedback and face-to-face feedback were used in tutor training events in Nottingham. These checklists can be found in Chapter 3 'Assess your own teaching quality' in Race and Brown's book. These offer a list of statements with the aim of making tutors more conscious of good assessment practices. The list includes statements such as:

> 'I correct errors in work, but not to the extent of demoralising learners' (Race and Brown, 1995: 60)

and:

> 'I ensure that each face-to-face feedback episode concludes on a positive note, and that learners leave with a smile where possible!' (Race and Brown, 1995: 64)

In most written work monitored, the correction consisted of wavy or straight lines under words or sentences and ticks around the edges of students' texts. It remains doubtful if this is helpful or purposeful. In order to help students to understand corrections, tutors should introduce marking symbols such as *sp* for *spelling* especially when written work is assessed. These symbols should be standardised in any one institution (see Appendix 5, p124) which would save valuable contact time as students can self-correct or re-write their piece at home. In order to improve their performance, they could identify their weaknesses or carry out peer-marking if appropriate.

However, it can be argued that work done by adult learners should only be corrected and not marked. Some tutors have shown first attempts to give marks, e.g. scores out of twenty or two marks per correct answer. (German Stage 1, 1996/97 Nottingham and Italian Stage 4, 1996/97, Nottingham)

Marking would contradict the declared aim to keep assessment and accreditation low key and contradicts the notion of diagnostic assessment as Ainslie and Lamping state:

> 'An evaluation is a value judgement made after an assessment exercise has been carried out; it is also what teachers do when they consider how successfully a lesson went. Evaluation is descriptive of progress and strengths and weaknesses; it does not usually include marks or scores.' (Ainslie and Lamping, 1995: 4)

Opting for marks or scores would mean that an element of competition is introduced and this might have an adverse effect on the benefits of assessment, i.e. students evaluate their own progress and diagnose their own strengths and weaknesses. Therefore it is advisable to introduce scores or marks only if the group as a whole or if individual learners specifically ask for it.

> ### Assessment Principle 11
> Assessment should be **valid**, i.e. it should assess what it sets out to assess.

Discrepancy in the assessment task and the skill which it is aiming to assess were mainly found in tutors' attempt to test learners' oral skills. Quite common were for example exercises in reading aloud in order to assess the skill of speaking (Spanish Stage 1, Nottingham, Italian Stage 3, Matlock, French Stage 4, Matlock, Welsh Stage 1, Nottingham, Russian Stage 5, Nottingham, Russian Stage 5, Alfreton, all 1996/97). These exercises — done during the contact hours or at home — might be beneficial for the development of correct pronunciation and intonation which are often neglected in language courses. Reading aloud certainly does not assess the communicative skill as is indicated by Ainslie and Lamping:

> 'There seems little justification for including in adult classes today techniques such as reading aloud a prepared passage.' (Ainslie and Lamping, 1995: 25)

Furthermore, the methods used for testing the skill of speaking were short of variety, flexibility and realism which is rather surprising as the nature of adult language courses lends itself to communicative activities as adults tend to welcome social interaction within the group. Some tutors opted for rehearsed dialogues provided by coursebooks. Sometimes the communicative assessment consisted of an audiocassette recording of 60 minutes of oral activities going on in the classroom whereby no individual voices were recognisable. (Spanish Stage 2, Matlock, German Stage 2, Matlock, Italian Stage 1, Matlock, all 1996/97)

In most cases, the assessment tasks did not include some element of choice for the learner, there was no real interaction in the sense of opportunities for meaningful communication and the tasks were neither interesting nor challenging nor stimulating.

Audiocassettes, videotapes, picture prompts, posters, music and realia could be used to add more variety to tasks. The latter especially could be implemented to great effect to trigger question-answer sessions or guessing games. For instance, authentic objects related to Easter or Christmas could be brought into the session. The student task would be to discover what the object is made for, made of and used for, i.e. what this object tells us about the society and culture of the country of origin. The same applies to ordinary household items which are typical for the target country but unknown in the learners' home country.

Out of some 40 language tutors only one tutor used picture prompts for the assessment of speaking. (French Stage 2, 1996/97, Nottingham)

Only one tutor felt inspired by a tutor training meeting and subsequently offered students the choice of giving a short talk or writing a short text about their favourite object or possession. (Russian Stage 5, 1996/97, Nottingham and Alfreton)

It can be stated that — at least in the Nottingham case — tutors need more training especially in the assessment of the communicative skill. Tutor training meetings to that effect have therefore been implemented in Nottingham.

> ### Assessment Principle 12
> Assessment activities should be accompanied by clear and straightforward **instructions**.

If a positive introduction has led to positive attitudes towards assessment, it would be counterproductive to offer students a linguistic activity without giving them clear information about the structure of the activity, the techniques and materials which are going to be used. Race goes further and declares:

> *'Assessment needs to be transparent to students, staff and employers.'*
> (Race P in Knight P, 1995: 67)

The monitoring of linguistic assignments at Nottingham University showed that transparent and clear instructions are vital. In some cases it proved very difficult to figure out what a particular exercise consisted of, especially as far as listening comprehension tasks were concerned. Was the activity based on an audiocassette, on a videotape or on satellite TV? Did the tutor read the text aloud?

How often did the students listen to the sequence? How many minutes did the listening last? How much time was set aside for the students to write the answers? These are only a few questions. It might well be the case that tutors gave explanations and instructions face-to-face which is laudable. In the light of future teaching quality audits (TQA) in British institutions of higher education and with the presence of external examiners on university examination boards this will no longer be regarded as acceptable assessment practice.

Examples of insufficient or missing instructions were found in assessment activities of all four skill areas:

For **written** exercises there were no word or time limits given, there was no mention of the use of a monolingual or bilingual dictionary, no information about details to be covered apart from the occasional hint 'write a letter to the hotel asking for information (prices for instance) ... '. Sometimes it was not clear if the written work was a piece of free writing or if concrete guidelines, topic-related vocabulary, model sentences or model texts were provided by the tutor.

The moderation of **speaking** assessment had to be carried out without any information about the nature of the exercise, e.g. preparation of students, free speaking or rehearsed role play?

The recordings did not contain vital information about students' names, course title, date or academic year. The recordings were often of very poor quality due to sub-standard accommodation and equipment.

Listening comprehension tasks should state the source of the material used, the techniques applied and personalised instructions for the students, for example:

'You will hear a news broadcast from TV channel X lasting 2 minutes. You will hear the broadcast three times (3 x 2 minutes). The first time you should just listen to understand the gist of the broadcast. During the second listening you should concentrate on the details, take notes and answer the questions. The third listening gives you the chance to complete and check answers. After the third listening you will have 2 more minutes to double-check your work. Total time: 8 minutes. Please answer in complete sentences in the target language.'

> **Assessment Principle 13**
> Assessment activities should be accompanied by clear and transparent **assessment criteria** which should be known by the students before the assessment task is carried out.

No examples of the use of assessment criteria were recorded during the monitoring. This might have been the result of criterion referenced assessment where the results of the assignment activities are recorded as unsubmitted, satisfactory, unsatisfactory. However, the adult learner needs to know which components of the writing task will be central. This would give him or her valuable feedback on strengths and weaknesses and indicate the need for revision. For the oral presentation for instance, the skill factors could be accuracy, range of expression and vocabulary, content, structure and presentation skills. Students should be informed about the skill factors and their weighting in the overall assessment before they attempt the task. This would ensure that students receive feedback on strengths and weaknesses in specific areas of their oral performance.

Conclusion

One can conclude from the findings that there are clearly areas in need of development and training as most tutors are nowadays involved in the design and administration of the assignments. This is not surprising, as assessment and accreditation are new on the agenda, at least for tutors who come from a liberal adult eduaction background or tutors who have not been involved in examining. In the light of lifelong learning and learning banks, credit accumulation and credit transfer will become more and more widely accepted. For this we will need qualified tutors as well as comparable curricula and more standardised assessment procedures within the diversity of the current provision in the subject area.

A number of studies have been published by the Council of Europe modern languages project to that effect, for example *'Identifying the needs of adults learning a foreign language'* by Richterich and Chancerel (1980) and *'Developing a unit/credit scheme of adult language learning'* prepared for the Council of Europe by Trim (1980).

In order to achieve standardisation in learning and teaching of languages in adult education and mutual recognition of teacher training schemes, the International Certificate Conference (ICC) has developed together with their European partners and with the help of a subsidy from the SOCRATES programme (LINGUA) a *Framework for Teacher Training and Accreditation.* ICC is presently developing a new project *Train the trainer,* a course for trainers of foreign language tutors in adult education . . .

It can therefore be said that initial as well as continuous training in teaching and assessing adult language learners is not only desirable but crucial if assessment and accreditation are to play an important part in post-liberal adult education in future years to come. It is a daunting but ultimately extremely rewarding challenge.

Bibliography

Ainslie S and A Lamping, *Assessing adult learners* (CILT, 1995)

Ambrose P, G Holloway and G Mayhew, *All change! Accreditation as a challenge to liberal adult education* (Centre for Continuing Education at the University of Sussex, 1994)

Arthur L and S Hurd, *The adult language learner* (CILT, 1993)

Berndt A, 'Fremdsprachenlernen im höheren Erwachsenenalter. Ansätze zu einer Sprachgeragogik' in *Info DaF Vol 24, No. 1* (Germany: Deutscher Akademischer Austauschdienst in Zusammenarbeit mit dem Fachverband Deutsch als Fremdsprache, 1997)

Bianchi M, B Busch B and P Sommet, *Partnerschaftliches Lernen im Fremdsprachenunterricht* (Germany: Pädagogische Arbeitsstelle des Deutschen Volkshochschul-Verbandes, 1987)

Convery A and D Coyle, *Differentiation — taking the initiative* (CILT, 1993)

Higher Education Funding Council of England, *Circular 3/94 Continuing Education* (HEFCE, January 1994)

International Certificate Conference e.V., *A framework for ICC teacher training and accreditation* (Germany: ICC, 1997)

For more information contact the ICC, Hansaallee 150, 60320 Frankfurt/Main, Germany.

Knight P (ed), *Assessment for learning in Higher Education* (Kogan Page, 1995)

Minton D, *Teaching Skills in Further and Adult Education* (Macmillan Press Ltd, 1997)

Race P, 'What has assessment done for us — and to us?' in Knight P (ed), *Assessment for learning in Higher Education* (Kogan Page, 1995)

Race P and S Brown, *500 tips for tutors* (Kogan Page, 1993)

Race P and S Brown, *Assess your own teaching quality* (Kogan Page, 1995)

Richterich R and J-L Chancerel, *Identifying the needs of adults learning a foreign language* (Pergamon Press, 1980)

Trim J L M, *Developing a unit/credit scheme of adult language learning* (Pergamon Press, 1980)

The Open University, *Tutor Guide. L230 Motive: Moving on in German. A second level course. Tutor Guidance 1998* (The Open University, 1997)

8 Measuring the impact of accreditation: two surveys on the provision of modern languages in university departments of continuing education

Toni Ibarz, University of Sheffield
Marion Spöring, University of Dundee

This paper presents the background and the preliminary research that was used as the basis for the development of a system of accreditation of modern language courses in adult continuing education. As is often the case with research resulting from surveys, the next few pages hide a wealth of individual and group experiences that can only be presented in summary form. Many part-time students, hourly paid tutors and full-time university staff have made this paper possible. In a way they are all part of UACE Linguists, the group whose papers are gathered in this publication. A few approximate figures may help to give an idea of the size of the group. There are 25 universities with departments that would come under the category of CE (continuing education) where modern language courses are taught. The names vary, some of the terms used are: extramural, adult and/or continuing education, lifelong learning, etc. There are approximately fifteen full-time and ten half-time language specialists in such departments. Most of the teaching is done by over 500 hourly paid tutors with an estimated 12,000 to 15,000 part-time students.

UACE Linguists

The name chosen by the group reflects very well its context and its area of professional activity. In its web page, the Universities Association for Continuing Education (UACE) describes itself as an association that:

- promotes and represents the interests of continuing education within higher education;

- acts as a forum for the discussion of policy issues within higher education as they affect continuing education, and formulates policy accordingly;

- promotes and conducts research and disseminates the results of this research to the general public and interested organisations.

UACE has well-established links with the Funding Councils, the Department for Education and Employment, the Scottish Office, Industry, and Education Department, and the Committee of Vice-Chancellors and Principals, and is consulted regularly on CE issues. UACE has institutional representation on its Council from 93 Higher Education Institutions in the United Kingdom. The Chair of UACE is a member of the Committee of Vice-Chancellors and Principals.

UACE's main professional activities are conducted through a series of networks, with membership open to CE staff from any institution belonging to UACE, and through two annual conferences: one is on general CE issues and the other on continuing vocational education. Some of the networks are:

- Administration
- Continuing Education in Rural Areas
- Continuing Vocational Education
- Educational Equality
- Flexible Learning
- International
- Women and Continuing Education
- Work-based Learning.

UACE Linguists was formed in 1994 by members of the International Network Group (then known as the Working Party on Europe) who felt languages lacked representation and even visibility in the association. This lack of formalised presence was felt to be detrimental to the quality and status of language courses. At the same time, it was also felt that UACE might benefit from greater awareness of the opportunities offered in Europe and beyond which were linked to language use, learning and training. At that time UACE was mainly the association of the university departments of continuing education which existed almost exclusively in the old universities. UACE Linguists was, therefore, in its inception a very focused group, formed by the few full-time modern languages course directors that worked in university departments of CE. Such departments had a long tradition of liberal education and were also well established providers of continuing vocational education (CVE).

In England and Wales, modern languages as a subject with linguists employed as full-time course directors did not become established until the session 1989–90, when the responsible bodies, which had had a major impact in determining what could be taught in university CE since the 1944 Education Act, were removed. From then on CE departments were free to teach any subject. In Scotland changes concerning the funding of university CE were even more dramatic with the change of funding bodies and a considerable increase in resources (UFC circular 10/90) which, as in the rest of Britain, allowed for the creation of full-time posts in modern languages. The existence of university CE departments in England and Wales was thrown into turmoil when in May 1993, the Higher Education Funding Council (HEFCE), issued a circular (18/93) on the future funding of CE which placed emphasis on the accreditation of vocational and non-vocational CE courses. In many departments, language courses had just become established when the challenge of accreditation posed serious questions about their presence and their future in university CE. To respond to this immediate challenge and to raise the profile of modern languages in CE, UACE Linguists was formed.

When in 1989–90 the increased funding allowed modern languages courses to run on a more sound foundation, the number of courses increased and the impact of this new influx of students was considerable. By 1994 close to half the 36 or so existing university CE departments had appointed a full-time member of staff with responsibility for modern languages. And more significantly, in a few departments students on language courses represented between one fifth and one fourth of the total FTE (full-time equivalent) count, in one or two cases much more. The provision of courses varied considerably from department to department, from beginners to degree and even postgraduate courses, field trips, intensive courses, etc. There was also a wide range of languages which included minority and community languages. However, the great majority were beginners and intermediate classes, precisely the type of courses which, in terms of university accreditation, presented a greater challenge.

The first survey

Towards the end of 1993, to find out the type of information presented in the previous paragraph, members of UACE's International Network Group with an interest in modern languages had decided to initiate their collaborative activity with a survey which would hopefully give an overview of the nationwide provision of modern languages courses in departments of CE. As indicated above, it was also hoped that the survey would encourage co-operation among linguists in those departments at a time of major change.

The survey questionnaires were sent to the 36 universities across the whole of Britain which, according to the Education Authorities Directory, had departments of CE. There were 29 responses, among those five from departments which sent a brochure with their programme but did not complete the questionnaire, also four departments offered culture courses with perhaps only a small element of language. At the time, the extremely high rate of response was seen by some as a sign of the interest and commitment to the teaching of modern languages, others saw it as an indication of the concern as to the future of the courses. The information gathered referred to the academic Year 93–94.

The survey confirmed the diversity of provision among departments, which is not surprising considering the degree of autonomy of British universities. The 29 departments surveyed taught approximately 1,200 courses in modern languages between them. They varied greatly in number from department to department.

Number of courses	Number of universities
1–14	5
15–24	8
25–49	5
50–74	5
75–99	3
100–115	3

Many departments taught mainly the more widely taught languages, but a few saw their function as providers of courses on languages that would not normally be taught anywhere else. In some instances there was a clear effort to satisfy the needs of the local community as, for example, was the case of one of the colleges of the University of Wales where 64 Welsh language classes were being taught. The provision of non European languages was very patchy, although there were universities offering courses in languages like Amharic or Swahili. The high presence of Latin was perhaps unexpected, as was the fact that more departments taught Russian than Spanish as seen in Chart 1 (Appendix 6, p126), notwithstanding the number of courses and the number of students involved. Chart 2 (Appendix 6, p126) shows that most languages were taught below GCSE/Standard Grade level which was the boundary between intermediate and advanced level. Most respondents described their courses as liberal adult education, only 9% were either business or translation courses, the term undergraduate meant that the course was part of an undergraduate qualification.

The length of courses was another indication of the great variations between CE departments, to the extent that it could be said that no two departments had adopted the same pattern. The table that follows attempts to give an indication of the length of existing courses:

Majority of courses	Number of universities
10 hours	2
30 hours	1
36–38 hours	3
40–42 hours	7
46–52 hours	5
60 hours	4
Others	7

When questioned about the topics for discussion in the proposed UACE Linguists network, almost unanimously the preferred topic for discussion was accreditation, followed by the training of part-time language tutors, quality assessment, and approaches to testing and evaluation. As expected, the information gathered in the survey made possible the creation of a group in England and one in Scotland which immediately focused on overcoming the problems that hitherto had been confronted on an almost individual basis. The result was that by 1995 most departments had been able to accredit modern language modules at undergraduate level 1, often within a framework leading to a qualification such as a Certificate of Higher Education or a Certificate in Modern Languages. There had been an attempt to standardise the number of credits, length, content and assessment of the modules but the diverse traditions and demands of each institution had made this impossible. Another aim had been to devise an assessment scheme which incorporated as much as possible the views of part-time tutors and was not intimidating to students, this may have been another factor that limited the tendency towards standardisation. Some of the papers which follow will illustrate the type of assessment models that were developed by some of the members of this group.

Accreditation in the context of university CE departments

Circular 18/93 meant, therefore, that many CE departments which had allowed the growth of modern language provision simply because of the demand from students and because they were relatively easy to set up and run, had to find a framework for accrediting their language courses. This was not an easy task and, in common with other sectors where accreditation had been introduced, there was an issue of student resistance. However, other obstacles were unique to CE departments and most of them were related to their HE context and to the traditions of universities and their relationship with adult education.

Universities are awarding bodies and unlike other institutions can decide independently what they expect of students in exchange for credits. It became clear during discussions that the organisation and politics of language teaching differed substantially from institution to institution. The lonely full-time linguist in the CE department had to confront, to a greater or a lesser extent, some of the following or similar situations:

- academic and administrative staff in CE departments who had difficulties in understanding the specific requirements of modern languages and in some cases were not as supportive as they should have been;

- committees involved in the approval of the proposals at faculty and university level which did not contain any linguists;

- other modern languages teaching departments or units in the university which were not supportive of the proposals. In a few cases there was suspicion and even open antagonism;

- initially, a desire to bring languages into line with humanities subjects and an expectation that they would conform to the established model based on a combination of the traditional essay and the three-hour exam;

- later, a desire to create a system of assessment which mirrored exactly that of the conventional undergraduate courses, with an insistence on the same content, number of contact hours, number of pieces of assessment, etc, regardless of the needs of adult students.

The impact of accreditation: the second survey

Eventually, departments succeeded in having their proposals for accreditation approved and the need was felt to assess what the impact of accreditation on modern language courses had been. A second survey was suggested to update the data from the first. There was also a new factor that contributed to the desirability of further research. A new concern was preoccupying full-time academics: as a result of the Research Assessment Exercise, renewed pressure was being applied on CE staff to produce research, in spite of their onerous administrative and managerial burden. This was a determining factor in persuading UACE Linguists to organise the Nottingham conference and to turn it into a yearly meeting which would act as a catalyst for research.

The second survey, carried out during the first half of 1997, was less of a mapping out exercise than the first one and was more a follow-up study. Looking at the first survey and using our knowledge of developments in CE departments, a representative sample of six departments in Scotland and twelve in England and Wales were sent a questionnaire. Most questions focused on the impact of accreditation.

The second survey: England and Wales

By 1997, the rapid growth in language courses and in the appointment of full-time linguists to CE departments had come to a halt. However, it became apparent that there had not been a sudden change of attitude towards languages, there were no cases of major expansion or contraction in the programmes offered. Only two departments reported a substantial decrease in student numbers. Four other departments indicated that the number of courses had not changed but they were now running with fewer students.

When asked what the impact of accreditation had been on the modern language courses on offer, the answers were more positive than negative. They ranged from the slightly negative to the very positive:

We have had to build assessment into all courses and courses have become more formal and perhaps less relaxed.

Very slight; most students see learning a language as a 'test' in any case.

There has been very little impact overall, but of course there is more administration for clerical staff and tutors.

No visible impact, i.e. course numbers/student numbers. Problems with administration of credits, credit collection and 'storage'.

It's been a good discipline. It's tightened up our quality control in all areas. Our tutors are now formally approved and CVs centrally filed. The course proposals are more clearly drawn up. Teaching objectives clearly stated and assessment clearly stated and monitored. This has then fed through into staff development which has been quite intensive — but well-received.

Positive:
• more structured course planning
• standardisation of assignments set across languages and levels
• more feedback on progress to students
• bank of assignments now kept to show potential students the level of the class.

When asked about the response to accreditation by students, some of the representative comments were:

They were not very interested, but were not anti.

A few objected, the majority responded with good humour. Few students take it really seriously, but are happy to go along with it.

Mostly okay, depending on tutor's attitude / how they 'sold' it to their classes.

It depends on the tutor... An excellent tutor can sweep a whole group through assessment without the class really noticing...

Full-time language specialists indicated that part-time tutors were:

Fed up with extra paper work involved. Enjoyed the extra training sessions.

Scared but most tutors now very positive. We arranged specific training sessions.

The second survey: Scotland

Scotland has a long-standing university tradition and all 'old' universities have offered 'extramural' classes for many years, but some new institutions also offer adult education classes to the community. At the point of survey, there were fourteen HE institutions offering languages in their programmes. As referred to earlier, the increased funding of CE provision from 1990 onwards had allowed to employ linguists with CE responsibilities for the language programmes. The Scottish Higher Education Funding Council outlined its move towards the mainstreaming of adult and continuing education programmes in circular 53/94, which made a distinction between CPE (Continuing Personal Education) and CPD (Continuing Professional Development). This allowed SCOTCAT (Scottish Credit Accumulation and Transfer) based accreditation to be introduced to large parts of the existing programmes, depending on the provider. However, there is the recognition that not all parts of the programmes can be accredited and funding is available for non accredited courses.

As had happened in England and Wales, the need to address these issues led to the formation of a Scottish UACE Linguists' group, the main difference being that from the beginning it comprised linguists based in the old and new universities. The Scottish Survey, based on seven institutions out of the fourteen that had been approached, included a wider range of institutions, and highlighted the potential for delivering CE in modern languages from different departments:

- two institutions fully integrated their CE into an undergraduate programme which was delivered in mixed full-time and part-time mode by the mainstream department;

- three had a well established and independent language programme owned by departments of continuing education;

- one institution offered complementary language programmes, one based in the CE department, the other in a dedicated language;

- one had a programme taught by a mainstream department, marketed by a department of continuing education and delivered by distance learning.

With the exception of one institution, all HE institutions continue to offer community and less well subscribed languages. In most institutions this happens on a non-accredited basis, although financial implications are mentioned like higher enrolment fees for non-accredited courses, cross-subsidies and policies for the maintenance of less subscribed languages.

The issues identified were largely similar to those mentioned in the survey for England and Wales:

- increased bureaucracy and workload for programme co-ordinators, clerical and tutoring staff;

- increased demand for staff development for all part-time tutors;

- the need for the guidance for students in general, a clearer path of progression for students and part-timers.

Two respondents mentioned initial hostility of students towards accreditation, fearing unequal treatment in the classroom, faster pace, unsuitable content/syllabi for older learners, etc. These worries, however, did not seem to materialise following the introduction of assessment. Younger learners in general seemed to be more positive towards assessment in general. A positive impact on teaching was also mentioned. Quotes from questionnaires from two different institutions may serve to summarise the attitude of many staff:

> We have tried to ensure that accreditation has had as little impact as possible on what we would consider appropriate course design for the type of group we are dealing with. A lot of work has to be put into reassuring and communication with students. The main consequence has been bureaucratic and financial.

> A lot of training has been required for tutors to produce intended learning outcomes and to ensure that they do all that is required of them administratively. Given the limited time they have with us and given our limited resources to pay them for training, I feel that this has taken away from other areas of training such as methodology, for example. Generally tutors would rather not have to assess but are realistic about having to do it: they are a crucial variable in how it is perceived by students. A recent questionnaire showed most tutors to be aware of some advantages and some disadvantages in assessment. For, a worrying thing is that accreditation sometimes unjustly gets the blame for, e.g. poor teaching.

> The younger students (aged 18–30) accept the benefits of a certificate/SCOTCAT points; some mature students accept the benefits of assessment; others are put off by it.

As in England and Wales, a variety of accreditation models is in operation (opt in, opt out, no choice). Again, this reflects the differing approaches favoured by the different institutions, as is the nature of the assessment, number of SCOTCAT points awarded and comparability with mainstream courses within that institution.

The results of the survey were supported by the research carried out into student attitudes towards assessment by two CE departments. One study by Cooke, Mackle, Spöring (1996), focusing on student attitudes in accredited and non-accredited courses in one institution, particularly referred to languages. The survey also identified a desire to share in the initial training and continuing professional development of tutors and this will be the main topic of the next UACE Linguists conference held in Edinburgh in July 98.

Other issues of concern

The surveys dealt also with other issues which are not so directly relevant to accreditation. Very briefly, they were:

- the relative position of modern languages *vis-à-vis* other subjects offered in the department, where the great majority of replies detected no changes. The purpose of this question was to find out if CE departments were beginning to change their attitude towards the provision of language courses;

- the ability to continue offering community languages and the willingness to respond to the needs of minority groups, which had a very laudable tradition in some departments. Several respondents indicated that the changes in funding and the rush to accreditation had severely reduced this type of commitment;

- a question on plans to introduce new initiatives in the area of language teaching was met frequently with 'not for the time being, we are consolidating at present', 'there is no time for new initiatives';

- there was also a question of involvement in international/European projects. Almost all the respondents said they would like to be involved but that they were not;

- another area where CE departments have been weak in the past was in the provision of continuing vocational education, which is also an anomaly considering that many CE departments are very strong in CVE. There was no indication of a redressing of this imbalance. However, there are signs of a departure from programmes based exclusively on LAE type courses, for example some departments have been involved in CPD, mainly in programmes for linguists, training for part-time tutors and INSET for school teachers.

Conclusion

It is obvious from the evidence presented in the previous paragraphs that much has been achieved, north and south of the border, in terms of accreditation, and that flexibility and student needs have been taken into account within a framework that satisfies the requirements for quality assurance. An awareness of its origins, the information provided by the surveys, the experience of co-operation between institutions, and between students, hourly paid tutors and full-time members of staff within each institution have contributed to strengthening the presence of UACE Linguists in universities. It is hoped that modern languages will continue to play an important role in opening the resources of the universities to their local communities and that the information provided in this paper will contribute to future developments.

Bibliography

Cooke A, K Mackle and M Spöring, 'Sleeping at the back. Student attitudes towards accreditation' in *Scottish Journal of Adult and Continuing Education* (1996)

European Commission White Paper Teaching and Learning: towards the learning society (http://www.cec.lu/en/comm/dg22/dg22.html)

HEFCE Circular 18/93 'Continuing Education', May 1993

http://www.stir.ac.uk/epd/uace/default.htm

Hübner A, 'Assessment and accreditation for languages — the emerging consensus?' in *Netword* (CILT, Autumn 1997)

Ibarz A, *Survey on provision of modern languages in university departments of continuing education: summary of results* (DACE, University of Sheffield, 1994)

Scottish Higher Education Funding Council (SHEFC) circular 53/1994

Universities Funding Council, 'Funding for Continuing Education 1990/91', circular 10/90

Appendix 1

Spanish Level 2: Assessable learning outcomes

Intended Learning Outcome 1

Students should be able to ...

A Talk about some of the things they did on the day prior to the class

- Say at what time they got up, had breakfast, went to work, did their homework, went to bed, etc.
- Say if they watched television, went out, went to the pictures, met friends, etc.

B Tell the story of their life so far

- Say where they were born, when they left school, where they worked, when they first went to Spain, when they got married, had children, etc.

C Talk about a holiday they once had with friends

- Say where and when they and their friends went on holiday, what they all did (collectively and individually).

Criteria *for a Pass*	Students should be able to communicate at least four different pieces of information and ask two questions. Students pass provided they can make themselves understood.

Intended Learning Outcome 2

Students produce a piece of written work (roughly 150 words) similar to the following ...

- For International Adult Learners' Week you have been chosen by DACE to attend a European conference on the difficulties facing adults who are trying to learn a new language. You have been asked to provide a brief biography for the conference publicity. Write out your main biographical details mentioning past visits to Spain with friends and/or family and how this made you want to learn Spanish.

- You are a Christian who believes in life after death: imagine you get to the Pearly Gates and St Peter asks you the story of your life to see whether or not he feels you should get into heaven. Write out the dialogue which takes place between yourself and St Peter.

Criteria *for a Pass*	Students pass provided they can communicate ten different pieces of information relating to the assignment.

Intended Learning Outcome 3

Students should be able to ...

A Talk about what they used to do when they were ten years old

Say where they went to school, what they did at the weekends/in the evenings, at what time they went to bed, if they did any work in the house, etc.

B Talk about what was happening at a particular moment in time (e.g. last Saturday at 10pm)

Say where they were, who they were with, what they were all doing.

C Talk about what the world will be like in 5/10/15 years from now

D Talk about good things and bad things that have happened this year

Criteria for a Pass	Students should be able to communicate at least four different pieces of information and ask two questions. Students pass provided they can make themselves understood.

Intended Learning Outcome 4

Students produce a piece of written work (roughly 150 words) similar to the following ...

- As a school project, your ten-year-old son/daughter has to compare his/her own life with that of his/her parents when they were young. He/she comes home and asks you what life was like for you when you were his/her age. Write out the dialogue which takes place between you both.

- You are suspected of having committed murder on Saturday night. Write out a statement for the police explaining what you (and friends/witnesses) were doing between 8 and 9pm on Saturday to prove that you couldn't have been the murderer.

- You went to a fortune teller's yesterday: write out the dialogue that took place between the fortune teller and yourself.

- You are a controversial newspaper columnist. Write out your column for 31 December, passing comment on what has been good/bad about the past year.

Criteria for a Pass	Students pass provided they can communicate ten different pieces of information relating to the assignment.

For Intended Learning Outcomes 1 & 3, students should be assessed in any one part (A, B, C or D). As part of each assessment activity, 'talk about' includes:
- listening to Spanish and making appropriate responses;
- asking questions of others.

For Intended Learning Outcomes 2 & 4, students should receive a piece of written Spanish which serves as a stimulus for their work.

Appendix 2

Questionnaire on the use of translation

UNIVERSITY OF BIRMINGHAM – MODERN LANGUAGES UNIT

Do you ever use translation to assess language competence? ☐ No ☐ Yes
If your answer is 'No', please explain why.

_____

_____

If your answer is 'Yes', please read on.
At what level(s) do you use translation in language testing?

_____

_____

What type of textual materials do you use?
☐ individual sentences
☐ paragraphs
☐ unabridged texts
☐ other _____

What are the sources from which you select the above materials?
☐ textbooks
☐ written by yourself
☐ realia
☐ other _____

If you use realia, which is the most frequent text genre?
☐ literature
☐ advertising
☐ magazines
☐ newspapers
☐ other _____

What, in your view, is the specific benefit of using translation as a means of testing language competence?

_____

_____

Many thanks for your co-operation.

Personal statement
of learning

UNIVERSITY OF NOTTINGHAM
School of Continuing Education
14–22 Shakespeare Street, Nottingham NG1 4QF
PERSONAL STATEMENT OF LEARNING

Name: .... **Title of course:** . FRENCH STAGE 2 YEAR 2 .....

Tutor: .... **Venue: UAEC, Shakespeare Street, Nottingham**

Session: 11/09/96-97... **Day & time of class:** . WED. 1.30. - .3.00pm .....

---

1 Personal learning outcome

Please use this space to describe what you think you have gained from this course. Include any thoughts you may have about your overall achievement, and about your progress and development.

I have continued to learn more about the French language, especially the use of the different tenses of the verbs.

With plenty of opportunity to practise spoken French in the class, I have gained some confidence in the use of the language.

---

2 Progression ... what next?

Now that you have completed this course, what might you go on to next? (e.g. another extra-mural course; another type of study; membership of a society; new employment, etc).

I hope to be able to continue learning French next year.

3   Learning outcome achieved

As a result of the knowledge and understanding you have gained on this course, *how far do you now feel able to*:

	I'm working towards this (✔)	I feel I have achieved this (✔)	and I think I demonstrated this achievement through (†)
Greet people in both formal and informal situations		✔	10
Introduce yourself and others in formal and informal situations		✔	10
Talk about yourself, your family and your professional life, using both the present and past tenses		✔	10
Talk about future plans		✔	10
Make arrangements for an evening out		✔	
Accept and reject invitations		✔	4
Ask for information by phone and letter about an area you wish to visit		✔	
Make arrangements for accommodation and transport		✔	
Say what you like to do in your leisure time	✔		4
Understand certain articles from the French press, and be aware of social trends with regard to leisure and holiday activities			
Compare aspects of French with aspects of the English language	✔		
Compare aspects of the French lifestyle and culture to aspects of British life and culture	✔		
Actively participate in lessons conducted almost entirely in French		✔	
Evaluate personal progress		✔	

(†) If you can, please make a note of how you demonstrated your achievement. Identify the activities you were involved in during the course whereby you were able to confirm your achievement, and note down the number(s) in the right hand column above.

1	a short talk to the class	6	personal study or project	11 making a tape recording 16 practical work/experiment
2	a demonstration to the class	7	homework task	12 a quiz/questionnaire 17 simulation/role play
3	helping others in the class	8	keeping a log/diary	13 class discussion 18 a group project
4	written work	9	critical reading	14 working in a small group 19 an exhibition of class work
5	an item you have made	10	giving oral answers	15 activity on a trip/visit 20 a group publication

4   Course Evaluation

Please use this space to comment on any aspects of the course and/or of the teaching.

Because this French course does not rely on the use of a text-book, but on input from the tutor, it is able to satisfy the needs of the students and continues to remain stimulating and interesting.

Do you wish this form to be returned to you? ..... NO ...... YES/NO
If you require this form to be returned, please attach a self-addressed envelope.

Appendix 4

Course syllabus

THE UNIVERSITY OF NOTTINGHAM
Department of Adult Education
14–22 Shakespeare Street, Nottingham NG1 4FQ

Courses Leading to the Certificate in Extra-Mural Studies
COURSE SYLLABUS

Tutor: . . . .

Title of Course: . . . .   C'EST MAGNIFIQUE! – French – Stage 1 . . . .

Day and Time of Class: . . .   Monday, 6.00 – 7.30 pm . . . .

Starting Date: . . . .   15 September 1997 . . . . . No. of Meetings: 18

Venue: . . . University Adult Education Centre, Shakespeare Street, Nottingham . . . . . .

Course Description/Syllabus

[Aims; significant topics; predominant teaching/learning methods, range of 'assignments' proposed and essential reading. Student learning objectives on reverse.]

Stage 1 is for people who have never studied the language before and who want to learn both the language and about the society and culture.

Aims

This course aims at developing speaking and listening skills together with reading and writing. The study of basic grammatical structures will be contextualised, ie integrated into a variety of basic everyday situations enabling you to cope either when travelling abroad, or for social contacts with foreign language speakers in your own country. It will heighten your awareness of a multi-lingual Europe. The course also aims to enable you to become an effective and autonomous language learner and communicator and will provide a sound basis for further study.

Course content

A selection of the following topic areas, including the appropriate language functions and the necessary grammar and vocabulary, will be studied (not necessarily in this order):

*   **Introduction to the course**
    Discussion about the course, textbook, self-assessment, syllabus and learning outcomes. Instructions in the target language.

*   **Personal Identification**
    Introducing yourself: name, address, telephone number, nationality, family members, occupations.
    Using the alphabet, spelling.

[Continued overleaf]

[Continued]

- **Self and others**
  Recap: Introducing yourself, giving information about yourself
  Introducing others
  Greeting people (formally and informally)
  Socialising when meeting people
  Expressing like and dislikes
  Enquiring about likes and dislikes

- **House and home**
  At home
  Describing a house or flat and the room/rooms in it
  Describing furniture

- **Food and drink**
  Ordering meals in restaurants
  Currency and prices

- **Shopping**
  Obtaining food in shops and markets
  Buying clothes, shoes, souvenirs
  Asking for and commenting upon prices, quality, size and colour
  Paying for things bought

- **Getting around**
  Asking for, following and giving directions
  Sightseeing and places of historical/cultural interest
  Basic geography of the country

- **Travel**
  Seeking accommodation
  Booking a room
  Obtaining information about an area and its facilities
  Public transport
  Obtaining tickets

[Continued overleaf]

[Continued]

Linguistic skills to be covered
Counting
Telling the time
Talking about the weather

Revision of familiar topics and grammatical points at regular intervals

Learning and teaching methods
Communicative language learning methodology
You will be encouraged to participate actively and opportunities will be given to practise the language through role-plays, simulations as well as through group work and pair work. You will be given guidance in choosing linguistic activities which you feel will assist you with your learning. These activities may include communicative games, listening comprehension exercises, reading comprehension tasks, writing tasks, independent work, e.g. work done at home or in the language laboratory.

The target language will be used as much as possible during the session and you will be encouraged to use the language whenever possible from the beginning of the course.

Assignments and accreditation
Assignments are an integral part of the course and have the important function of giving students and tutors detailed feedback about the progress and helping to identify areas which might required further study or revision. You will be encouraged to submit four pieces of coursework which will be assessed, each one reflecting one of the 4 linguistic skills i.e. speaking, listening, reading, writing.

Assignments and accreditation are requirements for all University Continuing Education Courses. Students completing the assessment activities and the PSL form are awarded credits (number depending on the length of the course) as part of the University's accreditation system.

Textbook and materials
To be announced.
Students are expected to obtain a copy of the textbook.

Authentic multi-media materials e.g. realia, slides, poster, audio and video tapes, etc. will be used where appropriate.

[Continued overleaf]

[Continued]

Student Learning Objectives/Planned Learning Outcomes:
As a result of the knowledge and understanding you gain on this course, you should be able to:
- Use appropriate social greetings
- Ask for and provide personal and family details
- Ask for and provide information about personal likes and dislikes
- Seek and give information in simple everyday situations
- Ask a speaker to repeat or slow down or spell a word
- Use and comprehend numbers correctly
- Ask for, give and respond appropriately to simple directions
- Read and comprehend a variety of short texts written in the target language
- Comprehend and use basic grammar rules correctly
- Produce short pieces of writing in the target language
- Attempt correct pronunciation and intonation of the target language
- Comprehend the target language as spoken by a native speaker
- Contrast and compare aspects of the country's life and culture with your own
- Compare aspects of the target language with aspects of English

Add any others you would like to learn or find you are learning during the course.

Signature: .... Date: ....

Return to Subject Specialist with completed Booklist [FORM C] and Personal Statement of Learning [FORM D] with Learning Outcomes completed.

For Office Use only:

Subject. Sp	RO	Lincoln	Library	File

Appendix 5

Error analysis

1   Each correction sign stands for a different category:

✓	=	positive feedback (good argument, well done)
^	=	word(s) are missing
?	=	meaning not comprehensible, not logical
( )	=	word(s) not necessary, superfluous

A   =   Agreement
- subject-verb-agreement
- pronoun-noun
- article-adjective noun
- pronouns and possessives within and across sentence boundaries
- verbs in relative clauses

Acc =   accent wrong or missing; *where applicable*

Art =   article (zero article, definite and indefinite article)

D   =   Declension (nominative, accusative, genitive, dative case); *where applicable*
- after preposition
- after verbs

G   =   gender (feminine, masculine, neuter); *where applicable*

Gr =   grammar

M   =   mood (indicative, subjunctive)

P   =   punctuation

Pl =   wrong plural form

Prep=   wrong preposition

R   =   repeated error

Sp =   spelling

T   =   tenses (tenses, active and passive voice)

W   =   wrong word(s) used

WO =   word order

2   Correction signs should be written on the space round the edges of the text.

3   Underlining:

——— =   error
⌣ =   not correct, but acceptable

4   **Tutor's comments** should be written in English, giving useful and encouraging feedback on the feedback sheet.

Lightening the tutor's workload

- please type or word process your work, or at least write it legibly
- please type, print or write double-spaced
- please leave ample space round the edges of your text for comments and corrections
- write your name and address at the top of the first sheet of paper and repeat your name on every new sheet
- number the pages
- use staples rather than paper clips
- *hand in your work on time*

Types and levels of courses

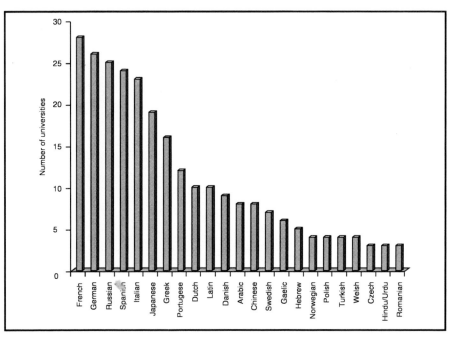

Chart 1: Number of CE departments teaching the most commonly taught languages (regardless of number of students or courses in each department)

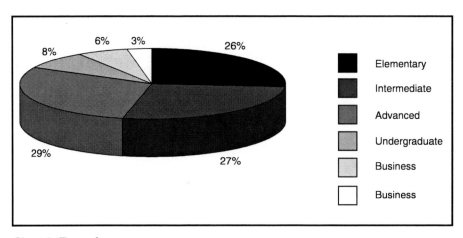

Chart 2: Type of course